D0821140

# Latin American Democracies

# Latin

# American

# Democracies

**Colombia, Costa Rica, Venezuela**

*John A. Peeler*

*The University of North Carolina Press*

*Chapel Hill and London*

© 1985 The University of North Carolina Press

Manufactured in the United States of America

Library of Congress Cataloging in Publication Data

Peeler, John A.

  Latin American democracies.

  Bibliography: p.

  Includes index.

  1. Representative government and representation—
Colombia. 2. Representative government and representation
—Costa Rica. 3. Representative government and represen-
tation—Venezuela. 4. Liberalism—Colombia. 5. Liberalism
—Costa Rica. 6. Liberalism—Venezuela. I. Title.

JL2881.P42  1985     321.8'098     84-13209
ISBN 0-8078-1634-5

# Contents

# Tables and Figures

# Preface

THIS STUDY is written in the spirit of the postbehavioral movement in political science. Probably the most important characteristic of this movement is its insistence on the inevitability and desirability of a concern with values in the study of society and politics. On one hand, postbehavioralism insists that even the most ostensibly "objective" research has value implications of which the researcher should be conscious, implications related to the choice of subject and method, the interpretation of data, the character of models, and the use of results. Critics have charged behavioralist political science with an often unwitting defense of injustice in the guise of empirical generalizations (see, for example, McCoy and Playford, 1967). On the other hand, postbehavioralists have insisted that a value commitment to justice or human liberation is not only an inevitable attribute of social science research but a desirable one (for example, Bay, 1965).

The critical theory of Jürgen Habermas represents the most sophisticated elaboration of the approach to social science research exemplified by postbehavioralism (see Habermas, 1971, particularly the appendix, pp. 301–17; and Bernstein, 1976, pt. 4). It would be presumptuous to say that this book systematically follows Habermas, but certainly my reading of Habermas (and Bernstein) has been exceedingly influential in shaping my conception of the task and proper conduct of social science research.

Key aspects of Habermas's thought can be presented here only in the most schematic form—the interested reader should refer to the cited texts. He argues that all knowledge is constituted by some human interest: inquiry in pursuit of knowledge is possible insofar as it is related to one of three problems of human existence. *Empirical-analytical* inquiry incorporates a *technical* interest in control of an objectified environment. *Historical-hermeneutical* inquiry proceeds by seeking understanding of the meaning of language as an embodiment of tradition between humans; the analyst therefore is necessarily involved in the communication process, a search for consensus or common meaning which may orient action. Thus, Habermas argues, historical-hermeneutical inquiry incorporates a *practical* interest. Finally, *critically oriented* inquiry analyzes human existence to determine when human relationships can be freed of unnecessary dependence or exploitation. It therefore incorporates an *emancipatory* interest, a thrust to free human beings from all that restricts the autonomous and responsible development of their human potential.

Each of these types of interest is identified with different spheres of human existence. Technical interest, related to empirical-analytical inquiry, is manifested in the world of work. Practical interest, related to historical-hermeneutical inquiry, is manifested in the world of language. And emancipatory interest, related to critically oriented inquiry, is manifested in the world of power.

The emancipatory interest in autonomy and responsibility is also directly manifested in language, our most distinctly human attribute. The practical interest of historical-hermeneutical inquiry deals with language as it is, with communication and action in an imperfect world. The emancipatory interest seeks to create the conditions for unconstrained communication. Habermas argues that all language presupposes the intention of universal and unconstrained consensus, that is, the intention that each person be autonomous and responsible. Language presupposes, in effect, what he calls an "ideal speech community," but such a community can be realized only in a society emancipated from the violence and exploitation that prevent individuals from expressing themselves autonomously and responsibly. This study is undertaken in the spirit of critical inquiry, informed by an interest in human emancipation.

This book insists that political systems are best understood as they develop dynamically through time. Thus the question of how a liberal democratic regime was established in each of three cases is analyzed through the interplay of forces and decisions in history. This longitudinal approach may be contrasted with a cross-sectional approach which compares countries with varying levels of democratic development at one point in time in order to yield generalizations about the correlates of democracy. Cross-sectional analyses have the virtue of allowing us to compare the relationships between similar variables in large numbers of countries. On the other hand, since human beings and human institutions exist and change in time, generalizations about them at one point in time have, in principle, limited utility for other times. The fullest understanding of political and social phenomena thus must make use of the time dimension.

The approach taken here combines two sometimes antagonistic tendencies in modern social science: political economy and political choice. Political economy as it is used here means the systematic analysis of the complex interactions of economic, social, and political phenomena. It assumes that political phenomena are in fundamental ways shaped or conditioned by their economic and social contexts; to that degree, the political realm is not autonomous, but rather shaped by its environment. At the same time, decisions shaped or avoided in the political realm have important economic and social consequences which may involve the most fundamental issues of justice and social power; therefore, the content of economic and social policy is an essential focus of the scholar of political economy. It should be obvious that this approach to political economy is very far from those versions that postulate a direct and one-sided economic determinism. Rather, it assumes that human social existence is complex, and must be understood as such.

A key conclusion of this study is the importance of elite

accommodation in the establishment and maintenance of stable liberal democracies in Latin America. Elites have been shown to have had considerable scope for maneuver and decision; liberal democracy in Latin America cannot be explained by exclusive reference to economic and social determinants. On the other hand, political choice is inevitably constrained by history and environment, so that one may not adequately understand a political situation without reference to such unchangeable factors. This book strives for an intelligent balance (such as that struck in Almond et al., eds., 1973).

As is usually the case, there are far more people to whom I am grateful than I can thank in this space. Many colleagues and students at Bucknell University have helped in diverse ways, most notably my good friends in the Department of Political Science and in the Program in Social Theory and Human Action, who taught me much and read my work with a critical eye. Students in several of my classes helped me hone my ideas, and my friends in the Bucknell Progressive Caucus have inspired and excited me to sharpen my political commitments and to relate them more directly to my scholarly work. Bucknell University made the whole enterprise possible by its support for sabbatical leaves in 1973–74 and 1981. Linda Danowsky typed the manuscript, skillfully and efficiently as always. I have benefited from the thoughtful comments of two anonymous readers for the University of North Carolina Press and have had the professional help of Iris Tillman Hill and the editorial staff of the Press.

Colleagues at several institutions in Latin America have provided invaluable facilities, encouragement, and criticism. I would single out Gabriel Murillo, Dora Rothlisberger, and the staff of the Departamento de Ciencia Política, Universidad de los Andes, Bogotá; José Agustín Silva Michelena, Heinz Sonntag, and the staff of the Centro de Estudio del Desarrollo, Universidad Central de Venezuela;

Charles Denton and the staff of the Instituto de Estudios de Población, Universidad Nacional de Costa Rica; José Luis Vega Carballo; and Roberto de la Ossa.

Among colleagues in the United States, I should particularly like to acknowledge the help of John Martz, Enrique Baloyra, Harvey Kline, Lars Schoultz, John Booth, Mitchell Seligson, Arturo Valenzuela, Robert Terry, and David Myers.

I affectionately greet my parents, Jay and Eileen Peeler, who made me what I am, and who may wonder where they went wrong after they read this book. My children, Beth and Jim, have had the good grace to enjoy and learn from our trips to Latin America and to tolerate my prolonged obsession with this book.

Judith Harris Peeler, my life companion, with her endless zest for adventure and infinite resourcefulness, has contributed not only to this enterprise but to my life in so many ways I could not recite them. I dedicate this work to her, with love.

If, in spite of all this help, I have not been able to avoid errors or shortcomings, I willingly accept the blame.

# Latin American Democracies

# I

*The Theory and
Practice of Liberal
Democracy*

THE DEMOCRATIC ETHOS, the notion that in some sense the right to rule a society should be based upon the consent of the ruled, has dominated the political life of the twentieth century throughout the world. The power of this idea is of course evident in the great democracies of the advanced industrial countries. Its influence is also to be found in the demand of Marxism and Leninism for economic as well as political democracy. The right of a people to self-determination, so critical in determining the shape of the contemporary international system, is at its root partly a democratic idea (though, admittedly, it also has predemocratic connections to the idea of sovereignty). The power of the ethos is attested by the fact that very few governments in the late twentieth century neglect to clothe themselves in formal democratic garb (for example, constitutions, parties, elections), even when these institutions are manifestly fraudulent. To openly flout the aspiration for democracy effectively undermines the legitimacy of almost any regime in the twentieth century, and thus opens it to opposition attack.

Yet there is no little irony in talking about the dominance of the democratic ethos in the century of Hitler, Franco, Stalin, and Pinochet. In the West we commonly distinguish between "true" democracies (for example, France, the United States) and fraudulent democracies (for example, the Soviet Union, South Africa), which prostitute democratic symbols. Most countries, of course, fall between these extremes, but we usually do not see countries outside the North Atlantic and Anglo-Saxon areas as full-fledged democracies.

There is irony too, as Westerners are increasingly aware, in calling our own political systems democracies when they seem to depend for their stability on the persistence of economic inequality and popular apathy. Are we not then presumptuous in condemning the excesses of "less democratic" regimes?

Those who have suffered imprisonment and torture usually do see a difference. The conventional concept of democracy emphasizes citizen rights and liberties which, to the extent they are respected, guarantee that persons will not be arbitrarily abducted, tortured, and murdered by the authorities. In many parts of Latin America today, the realization of even that part of the democratic canon would be a major gain; there it makes sense to work for the establishment of democracy, with all the imperfections we know only too well.

This is a book about democracy in Latin America. It starts with the assumption that democracy is a good thing (albeit imperfect). It seeks to convey an understanding of the economic and political conditions that allowed for the emergence and maintenance of stable democracies in three exceptional countries (Colombia, Costa Rica, and Venezuela). And it seeks to begin the task of thinking about how democracy as we know it—in Latin America and elsewhere—can transcend its internal contradictions and move beyond being simply an unusually pleasant mode of being dominated. We begin with democratic theory itself.

## Liberal Democracy: Liberal Essence and Democratic Legitimation

In this study *liberal democracy* refers to a political system in which (1) virtually all adult citizens are entitled to vote; (2) major policymaking officials are selected by the votes of citizens in elections in which more than one candidate has a reasonable chance of victory; and (3) there is substantial freedom for citizens to organize or join political parties and interest groups and to act individually or collectively to influence public policy (cf. Lively, 1977; Pennock, 1979). This definition corresponds closely to conventional twentieth-century usage, but it is important to remember that when we speak of democracy this way, we apply the label to a system that is very far from true "rule by the people." The following pages will argue that liberal democracy is essentially a liberal political system legitimated by the appearance of democracy (Macpherson, 1973 and 1977; A. Levine, 1981).

Liberalism as a tendency of economic and political thought emerged between 1600 and 1900 in a series of attempts to justify limitations on the right of government to interfere with the self-interested actions of individuals. Thomas Hobbes (*Leviathan*) helped to lay the philosophical foundation for liberalism with his emphasis on the individual in pursuit of self-interest as the basic unit of human life, and with the notion of the social contract between such individuals as the basis for society and the state. But the basic thrust of liberalism, from Locke to Adam Smith, to Malthus, and to John Stuart Mill, was toward limiting the state and enhancing the rights and liberties of individuals. The economic import of liberalism was the legitimation of free-enterprise capitalism through the argument that if all were free to pursue their economic interests, the whole society would be richer. Smith and the other classical liberal political economists rejected the notion that the state could legitimately or effectively define and enforce an authoritative concept of the public interest. The public interest could be better defined and served by the free interaction of private interests.

The thrust of political liberalism was basically congruent with that of economic liberalism in justifying the limited state and the maximization of individual liberties. From the victories over the Crown in seventeenth-century England, rationalized and defended by Locke, to the struggles for political rights central to the American and French revolutions, to Mill's defense of liberty and representative government, the liberal emphasis was on maximizing individual rights with respect to the state. Liberalism defended alike the economic freedom of enterprise and the political freedoms of speech, press, and religion. And as liberalism came to dominate thinking in the North Atlantic area after 1800, it was increasingly taken for granted that the state should respect and protect a broad range of economic and political rights of its citizens.

There were nevertheless unresolved tensions in liberal thought and practice. Economic liberalism was founded on the proposition that the state should respect the equal right of every individual to acquire and hold property and to use that property in order to acquire and hold more. Thus economic liberalism accepted extreme economic inequality in order to defend the rights of property. Political liberalism, on the other hand, from Hobbes and Locke on, was irreducibly founded in the proposition of the equality of all citizens. Whether basing their arguments on social contract (Hobbes and Locke), on convention (Hume), or on utility (Mill), liberals acknowledged no basis for the permanent superiority of one person over another. Governors should hold authority only by consent of the governed, and that authority in any case should not extend to violation of the rights of the governed (including very prominently the right to acquire and hold property).

Yet if every person is to have a truly equal right to property, is it not necessary to prevent concentrations of economic power (that is, property) which effectively foreclose access to property for the disadvantaged? And is it not also necessary to prevent concentrations of economic power in order to preserve meaningful political equality of citizens? In short, there is a tension between the liberal goal of maximizing individual liberty and the liberal postulate of equality.

A second area of unresolved contradictions, closely intertwined with the preceding difficulties, involves the scope of governmental authority. If government draws its authority from the consent of the governed (who are in principle equal), is it the first obligation of government then to do the bidding of the majority? Or is it rather to respect and protect the rights of citizens (including of course the rights of property)? Clearly, the point of liberalism (that is, to limit governmental authority and maximize rights of individuals) is potentially in conflict with its philosophical foundation in the consent of equal citizens. Democracy was from the beginning an unwanted but indispensable passenger on the liberal ship of state.

These philosophical inconsistencies were not so sharply perceived in the eighteenth and nineteenth centuries as they are today, and they proved no obstacle to the emergence of a liberal political and economic hegemony in the North Atlantic world. Liberal political economy justified and guided the progress of industrial capitalism, defending the concentration of capital and denigrating the propertyless masses as those who had failed for lack of enterprise. The states that administered industrial capitalism were increasingly liberal as well, though Germany and Scandinavia remind us that the commitment to liberalism was unenthusiastic. After the American and French revolutions the idea of society as a community of equal citizens gained increasing currency. The liberal states of the nineteenth century increasingly contrived to base the authority of their governments on the consent of the citizens, while at the same time limiting governmental authority and assuring that property and other rights would be protected.

James Madison, in his defense of the American Constitution, showed the way (*Federalist*, no. 10). John Locke had been preoccupied with guarding against monarchical tyranny and had used the notion of government by consent of the governed as a tool in that cause. A century later, Madison thought there was more reason to worry about tyranny of the majority. To put it more precisely, he feared that a government subservient to the poor masses might threaten the rights of men of substance. The Constitution sought to check both minority and majority tyranny, Madison argued, by means of the elaborate system of separation of powers and checks and balances within the federal government, which would work against any particular interest controlling the whole government. This end would be further served by the reservation of many powers to the states and by the sheer size of the federal union, which would make it exceedingly difficult for a permanent majority faction to form. If government by representatives of the people was the best barrier to minority tyranny, then the best means to prevent majority tyranny would be to set those representatives against one another, thereby limiting their aggregate power.

This concern to maximize the benefits of popular consent to a government while minimizing the risk of popular control was a central theme of nineteenth-century liberalism. There were certainly exceptions to this tendency: Thomas Paine comes to mind. But the dominant orientation was that of Alexis de Tocqueville and, later, John Stuart Mill. Tocqueville's great study *Democracy in America* was explicitly directed to the task of explaining to Europeans how this fearsome beast, democracy, actually worked reasonably well in America. Tocqueville was typical of European liberals in his simultaneous rejection of hereditary authority and his fear of the unwashed masses. He believed that democracy along the lines of what he found in Jacksonian America would inevitably come to Europe. So from that point of view perhaps his most significant finding was that democracy in America had not overwhelmed the great liberties on which the republic had been founded. Democracy, he thought, would surely require some adjustments of liberals, but it need not lead to the extinction of the liberal social order.

Mill went further, to actual advocacy of the democratization of the liberal political order. His argument was developed in *Representative Government*, on the basis of arguments in *On Liberty*, and his position was further extended in *The Subjection of Women*. Human capacities, Mill argued, are developed by their exercise. Thus misgovernment by an uninstructed majority could best be avoided in the long run by providing all competent adults with participatory opportunities through which they might develop their faculties. But note that Mill did not advocate majority rule.

He called for an elaborate system of plural voting for the educated minority which would enable the latter effectively to balance the numbers of the majority. The result would be a polity in which both educated minority and unlettered majority would be represented, but in which neither could predominate. The point, for Mill as for Madison, was not that the people should rule but that a liberal political order should be maintained with popular consent and participation. It is as if the liberal order were to be inoculated with the democratic virus in order precisely to guard against uncontrolled democratization.

There have been later elaborations (from T. H. Green to John Rawls), but after Mill the basic structure of the democratic legitimation of the liberal polity was in place. It guided and justified the progressive expansion of the franchise and the development of mass-based parties and groups which together have shaped the character of twentieth-century liberal democracy. This was the mainstream of Western political thought.

There were of course other streams. Rousseau, for example, unlike any liberal, took seriously and literally the meaning of democracy, "rule by the people." *The Social Contract* asked how a commonwealth could be constituted in which each person benefited by the protection and support of all others without surrendering any natural rights and liberties. His radical solution was that each person would surrender all such rights and liberties to a sovereign composed of all persons in the society. Thus each person would be completely subject to the will of the sovereign, but each person would also participate equally in sovereignty. The danger of majority tyranny could be averted if the people, acting as sovereign, thought not of their particular interests but only of the general interest (or "general will," in Rousseau's terminology). Rousseau thought it quite conceivable that individuals and minorities could be transfixed by their particular interests; in such cases the majority, activated by the general will, had a right to overrule them. But majorities, and even the whole people, might also depart from the general will to act in pursuit of particular interests. Faced with such a possibility, Rousseau could only offer the intercession of the divine lawgiver. Rousseau's system is thus beset by enormous tensions and difficulties. It nevertheless constitutes a uniquely rigorous attempt to specify what would be involved in a perfect democracy: rule of all the people by all the people.

Marx and Engels represent another current (see the *Critique of the Gotha Program*). They understood very clearly the role of the liberal state in administering and supporting the capitalist economy with a whole range of activities from poor laws to schools to protection of private property, and they recognized the importance of political as well as economic liberalism in justifying capitalism. So naturally they argued that the liberal state, with its increasing degree of democratic legitimation, could not be a genuine democracy because it deceived the workers into consenting to their own subordination and exploitation at the hands of the capitalist ruling class.

Antonio Gramsci made a major Marxian contribution to the theory of liberal democracy (1971), namely, the reinterpretation of the concept of *hegemony*. In conventional political analysis, hegemony and domination are taken to mean about the same thing: an asymmetrical relationship in which one or more persons rule over or control other persons. We use "hegemony" more or less conventionally in this book when we describe various nineteenth-century political patterns whereby individuals or parties were able to use combinations of force, patronage, or corruption to assure their control of the government over sustained periods of time. But our analysis of contemporary liberal democratic regimes in the region owes much to Gramsci's revision of the concept of hegemony. In political society (the state) the dominant class exercises coercive control or domination over the population. In civil society, or private life, the dominant class exercises control not coercively but ideologically: people consent to subjection because the intellectuals who control communication induce them to believe in the legitimacy of the established order. Gramsci labels this ideological control hegemony (see also Marcuse, 1964).

It was the genius of liberalism that liberal states were largely able to absorb these and other inimical intellectual currents, permitting their advocates to articulate them and to organize parties to advocate them. But the basic rules of the political game, the fundamental structures, were liberal: constitutional government, toleration of divergent viewpoints, competitive elections (to mention only a few). In Britain, France, or the Low Countries in the nineteenth century, well-entrenched liberal regimes induced socialists, conservatives, populists, and others to "work within the system," agreeing to tolerate their enemies in return for the assurance of toleration for themselves. Conservatives occasionally even took the lead in democratizing participation, in hopes of partisan advantage. But this simply emphasizes their acceptance of liberal institutions themselves. Since World War II, whether we look at Britain, France, Sweden, Italy, Germany, or the Netherlands, we see a fundamentally liberal political system, democratically legitimated, encompassing the peaceful competition of political forces from conservative to socialist. The same thing can be said about the United States as well, its truncated political spectrum notwithstanding. As Maurice Duverger (1974) has argued, this basic pattern of liberal democracy was taking shape during the nineteenth century and was largely in place by the beginning of the twentieth.

## The Practice of Liberal Democracy: Some Key Studies

Ever since political science emerged as a distinct discipline in the early twentieth century, one of its central preoccupations has been the study, interpretation, and defense of lib-

eral democracy. From Woodrow Wilson, A. Lawrence Lowell, and James Bryce to David Truman, Robert Dahl, and
Maurice Duverger, the focus has been on this peculiar historical construction, which itself came to maturity at about
the same time. Without attempting the impossible task of
surveying all of modern political science, the following
pages will try to convey a sense of what political scientists
have had to say about liberal democracy.

Most significantly, political science has already accepted
and propagated the use of the term "democracy" to label the
democratically legitimated liberal systems we have been
discussing. Thus from very early, the task of understanding
what democracy might be was relegated to the peripheral
field of normative theory, while the mainstream of political
science went on with the empirical enterprise of specifying
how this complex phenomenon we have come to call democracy works. Perhaps Joseph Schumpeter (an economist)
stated the position most directly when he argued that it is
an inaccurate picture of reality to say that the people in a
democracy determine policy (Schumpeter, 1962, chaps. 21–
22). In order to reflect what actually happens, we should,
he thought, define democracy as "that institutional arrangement for arriving at political decisions in which individuals acquire the power to decide by means of a competitive
struggle for the people's vote." This approach was certainly
shared by the political scientists before and after Schumpeter who shaped the pluralist perspective on the study
of democracy and the behavioral approach to the study of
politics.

Fundamentally, pluralism as developed by Robert Dahl
and others argued that modern democracy is characterized
neither by majority rule nor by minority rule but rather by
the competition for influence between many competing minorities. These minorities seek to enlarge their influence
relative to one another in order to secure a larger share of
the benefits dispensed through public policy. The people of
course have the opportunity to vote periodically for pub-

lic officials, and they also have the opportunity to enhance their influence over those officials by joining or organizing interest groups and political parties. Not everyone takes these opportunities, and those who do have more political power than those who do not. Government, in this model, has the relatively limited role of balancing and responding to the competing pressures upon it.

Behavioralism was the methodology of the pluralists. Behavioralists argued that it was possible and desirable to suspend judgments about what is good, better, and best in political life in order to get on with the task of accumulating data as building blocks for an objective, empirical, universal theory of politics. The theory to be constructed was to reflect observable political behavior as closely as possible and should systematically include or explain as much such behavior as possible. The focus, in short, was on using observable (preferably measurable) data to demonstrate associations and causal relationships in the world as it is. Behavioralism was thus a most appropriate method for the pluralist study of the actual practice of contemporary democracy.

The main impact of pluralist-behavioralist research was in confirming and elaborating what they expected to find in the area of mass attitudes and political behavior (Almond and Verba, 1963; Verba, Nie, and Kim, 1978; Cnudde and Neubauer, eds., 1969). In democratic systems generally, most citizens were found to be ignorant, apathetic, and inconsistent in their attitudes. Most people participate politically either not at all or only by voting, rather than seek out more demanding modes of involvement. Of course, significant differences between countries have been found, and some studies have questioned these generalizations on some points. Nevertheless, one of the main accomplishments of political science has been to cast doubt on the notion that democracy requires an informed, rational, and participatory public.

Other behavioral studies have focused on elites in executive and legislative positions, in parties, in associations, in bureaucracies (Parry, 1969). Pluralism presupposes that the real action in politics is between elites, and most behavioral research on elites either also assumes that or seeks to demonstrate it.

## The Evolution of Liberal Democracy: Some Key Studies

Several systematic attempts have been made to understand how the twentieth-century liberal democracies differ in their historical roots from less democratic systems. By far the most important such study is Barrington Moore's *Social Origins of Dictatorship and Democracy*. Moore seeks to explain how changes in social structure over long periods of time have led, in diverse societies, to democracy, fascism, and communism. The democratic systems considered are Britain, France, and the United States. He assumes familiarity with the German case of fascism and treats Japan in detail. Similarly, he assumes familiarity with Russia and treats China in detail as a communist case. Finally, he also considers India as an anomalous democracy in a country whose history and social structure do not fit his theory.

Moore regards economic classes as the main actors in social and political change. For the cases he studied, he argues that the evolving relationships between three classes have determined twentieth-century political outcomes. The three are the landed aristocracy, the bourgeoisie, and the peasantry. There are enormous differences between the three democratic cases, but Moore nevertheless contrives to argue that all three are characterized by the emergence to dominance of the bourgeoisie, by means of some sort of revolutionary upheaval. The other two key classes are held either to have come to terms with bourgeois interests or to have been eliminated as major forces. The emergence of liberal democracy is thus seen by Moore as a direct manifestation of bourgeois dominance and bourgeois interests.

Many of the criticisms of Moore's approach have come

from specialists on the particular countries he studied. For example, the North-South conflict which culminated in the American Civil War is held by Moore to be equivalent to a bourgeois revolution, but he must acknowledge that the great southern landholders cannot be thought of as a landed aristocracy in the European sense, nor can any class be found which corresponds to a European peasantry. In the British case the supposedly bourgeois revolutions of the seventeenth century turn out on close examination to be far more complex and distinguishing between bourgeoisie and aristocracy, far more difficult than Moore allows for. In France the peasantry were certainly not eliminated as a major force, and it may plausibly be argued that they also did not come to terms with bourgeois interests.

It would be impossible in this short space to summarize the numerous attempts to review and evaluate Moore's work. Suffice it to say that the book is still widely read and cited, but that it is in no sense regarded as definitive.

There have been other significant studies of the historical development of democracy. For example, Ralf Dahrendorf's study *Society and Democracy in Germany* is broadly consistent with Moore's argument, but much more detailed in its discussion of elements of the social structure and political culture of Germany which he maintains have obstructed the development of democracy there. Reinhard Bendix's *Kings or People* focuses entirely on democratization of European polities. Gabriel Almond et al., eds., *Crisis, Choice and Change*, Eric Nordlinger, *On the Autonomy of the Democratic State*, and Juan Linz and Alfred Stepan, eds., *The Breakdown of Democratic Regimes*, all emphasize, in contrast to Moore and Dahrendorf, the autonomy of political actors, particularly in crisis situations.

## *Measuring Liberal Democracy and Its Correlates: Macro-Comparisons*

If used critically, aggregate quantitative data and qualitative scales may provide a good starting point for comparisons between nations. There is a large body of such studies directed to determining the extent and correlates of political democracy. Two such studies exemplify what this method can and cannot do. Kenneth Bollen (1980) has recently developed a comparative index of political democracy which, he argues, is superior in scope and reliability to a number of earlier attempts comparatively to measure democracy. The index uses data from 113 countries in 1960 and 123 in 1965. It is based on six component scales, aggregated and standardized so that the minimum score is 0 and the maximum 100. The six components are as follows:

### *Political Liberties*

1. Press Freedom—degree of control normally exercised by any agency with the power to interfere with the dissemination and discussion of the news.
2. Freedom of Group Opposition—degree to which organized opposition is allowed (high = no parties excluded; low = no parties exist, or only one dominant party).
3. Government Sanctions—number of actions of government which curtail the political activities of one or more groups of the population (for example, censorship, curfew, and so forth).

### *Popular Sovereignty*

4. Fairness of Elections—degree to which elections are free from corruption and coercion (that is, free and competitive elections are most fair).
5. Executive Selection—is chief executive elected?
6. Legislative Selection—is legislative body elected, and how effective is it?

Each of these indices has been drawn from information contained in earlier studies. The reader need not be very perceptive to see that all are fundamentally based on some-one's judgment which has then been translated into an arbi-trarily constructed numerical scale. This is typical of stud-ies of this kind. The utility of the index depends on the willingness of readers to accept the judgments of the author and his sources. Further, even if these judgments are ac-cepted, one must be careful not to generalize beyond the particular time span covered by the study (in this case, around 1960 and around 1965). This sort of study is thus of very little use in assessing the stability of a regime. This is an important shortcoming in Latin America, where, as we have previously noted, many countries have episodes of something resembling liberal democracy, but few maintain them for more than a few years at a time.

Here are Bollen's scale values on the level of political de-mocracy in some countries:

| COUNTRY | 1960 | 1965 |
|---------|------|------|
| United States | 94.6 | 92.4 |
| Dominican Republic | 20.6 | 38.8 |
| Mexico | 80.1 | 74.5 |
| Guatemala | 69.8 | 39.5 |
| Costa Rica | 91.3 | 90.1 |
| Colombia | 69.7 | 71.4 |
| Venezuela | 72.5 | 73.4 |
| Chile | 99.7 | 97.0 |
| Argentina | 62.7 | 52.6 |
| Uruguay | 99.8 | 99.6 |
| United Kingdom | 99.3 | 99.1 |

Obviously, at a very general level the index does corre-spond to our intuitive sense of which countries were more democratic in the early 1960s. Just as obviously, it is subject to innumerable particular criticisms for placing country *X* above or below country *Y*. It is, in short, a blunt instrument, but not totally useless.

A different sort of macrocomparison is represented by Phillip Coulter's *Social Mobilization and Liberal Democracy* (1975). Coulter seeks not only a comparative measure of liberal democracy but also a measure of the association between level of democracy and level of social mobilization. It is thus an attempt to verify the theory that high levels or rates of change of urbanization, education, communication, industrialization, and economic development will be associated with democracy. Measuring democracy with indices of competitiveness, participation, and civil liberties, Coulter finds considerable confirmation of his hypothesis at the global level. A distinctive aspect of his study is that he then goes beyond the global study to examine the relationship on a regional level. Interestingly, his examination of the "Iberic-Latin" region (including Spain and Portugal as well as Latin America) in fact yields strikingly weak relationships between his indices of liberal democracy and those of social mobilization. Patterns that can be discerned at the global level simply do not appear in the Latin American context. Faced with the task of explaining why this is so, Coulter basically relies on the cultural analysis of Howard Wiarda (1973), that the deeply rooted corporatism of the Iberian tradition is inimical to liberal values, including liberal democracy.

## Criticisms of Pluralism and Behavioralism

Beginning in the 1960s, increasing numbers of political scientists and others directed criticisms at this pluralist-behavioralist mainstream of the discipline (McCoy and Playford, 1967; Skinner, 1973; Manley, 1983; Duncan, 1983). It was argued that the pluralist theory of democracy in effect justified and advocated, as well as describing, systems very far from the egalitarian and participatory ideals of democracy. It was pointed out that the pretension of pluralism to be a democratic theory hid a profoundly elitist bias. The tendency of behavioral research to look only at what is, and to generalize universally from that, was severely criticized on the grounds that it lent an aura of inevitability to situations that might well be changed. For example, popular apathy and ignorance might be far less frequent in a system in which participation was more meaningful. In short, both the underpinnings and the results of pluralism and behavioralism were cast into question. Also cast in doubt were the notions that democracy *is* liberal democracy, and that liberal democracy is the best possible political system.

The most systematic attempt to reconstruct democratic theory in light of these postbehavioral, antipluralist criticisms has been the work of C. B. Macpherson. He has argued in numerous works in recent decades that pluralism suffers from the same fatal inconsistencies that marked earlier forms of liberalism, flaws that effectively prevent its achieving the declared goal of liberation for all persons. He holds that liberalism from Hobbes on has started with a concept of human existence as necessarily a competition between individuals for possession of scarce benefits. Under the liberal concept of private property, possession of a good constitutes a right to exclude others from it, thus creating economic inequalities that negate the goal of equal rights and liberties with which liberalism begins. Liberalism, he argues, has not and cannot achieve either full liberation or democracy because its limited concepts of human nature and property block the way.

Macpherson then seeks to open up new possibilities by reaffirming and revising Mill's old emphasis on liberty and political participation as opportunities for the development of the human capacities or potential of each person. This leads directly to advocacy of a concept of property not as a right to exclude but rather as a *right not to be excluded* from the means of labor and self-development. These means are taken to include equal participation in decision-making about the allocation of resources in society. In effect, Macpherson is saying that if liberal democracy is to break through the limitations of pluralism and become more fully

democratic, it must break with capitalism and the possessive individualism that underlies it. Note, however, that
even Macpherson is not talking about democracy as "rule by
the people"; Macpherson is not Rousseau. When Macpherson discusses participatory democracy, the emphasis is on
full and equal participation as essential to development of
the human capacities of each individual. Democracy as rule
by the people collectively is not seriously discussed. We will
return to this issue in the final chapter.

## The Roots of Liberal Democracy in Latin America

Latin Americans were peripheral to the intellectual, political, and economic trends we have been discussing (Véliz,
1980; Belaúnde, 1966; Stein and Stein, 1970; Davis, 1972).
Spain and Portugal and their dependencies were scarcely in
the forefront of any of the great currents of the Atlantic
world in the eighteenth and nineteenth centuries. Theory
and practice in the Iberian empires remained fundamentally
at variance with the emerging liberalism of the West right
up to the struggles for independence. While in the West increasing efforts were made to limit and disperse authority,
the Iberians insisted on centralizing it. The great movement
to reduce the economic role of the state found scarcely an
echo in the Iberian world. The progressive erosion in the
sacred and secular authority of the church was actively resisted south of the Pyrenees. Thus the societies that evolved
in Iberia and its empires were the very antithesis of liberalism. The hegemonic position that liberalism would hold
further north remained with what Claudio Véliz has called
"the centralist tradition" in the Iberian world. Even popular
rebellions (for example, the *comuneros* in Nueva Granada or
the uprisings led by Hidalgo and Morelos in Mexico) frequently took the centralist form of demands for easing of
taxes and other oppressions.

However, those in Iberoamerica who opposed the hegemony of the peninsula frequently drew their inspiration from the emerging liberalism embodied in the Enlightenment, the American and French revolutions, and the new political economy. When the more educated upper classes took the lead in protests (as in Caracas, Buenos Aires, and Chile), they more often than not couched their demands in liberal terms: liberty, equality, government by consent of the governed, freedom of commerce. And when independence came, it established in every country of Latin America the liberal norm of constitutional government, including the expectation of periodic elections.

The liberal reformers of the early nineteenth century deceived themselves if they thought they could so easily be rid of the Iberian heritage. The social structure had been shaken and weakened to varying degrees (perhaps least so in Brazil, most in Venezuela), but nowhere had class relations fundamentally changed: everywhere a tiny landed and commercial elite retained the capacity to dominate and exploit the poor majority. In such a context the liberal values of equality and government by consent were scarcely more than rhetoric. In most countries violent seizures of power were legitimated and maintained by rigged elections, and civil wars often followed when the rigged elections were challenged. The formality of popular participation and consent masked the reality of control by segments of a small and usually fragmented elite. Meanwhile, the controlling elites used their power to safeguard opportunities to enrich themselves through trade with Britain and other metropolitan countries.

Yet it is too easy simply to dismiss these liberal institutions as vain fictions. No country went very long without a duly enacted constitution and formal elections of executive and legislative officials, even though it was understood that these exercises would normally be controlled. Formally liberal institutions became essential in Latin America in the nineteenth century, and they remain so today. There were several reasons for this.

First, given the liberal hegemony in the Atlantic world, many members of the Latin American ruling classes really believed that a good society was a liberal society, economically, politically, and culturally. To mandate formally liberal institutions was at least symbolically to move society closer to the ideal.

Second, even those Latin American elites who did not believe in liberal ideas still had to deal with leaders in the northern countries who did hold those values. A country that took the trouble to clothe itself in acceptably liberal institutions had some protection from the imperialistic arrogance of the "white man's burden" and "manifest destiny." A country whose government could not maintain order, and do so within forms seen as civilized by Europeans and North Americans, could not count on having its independence respected. Given the world hegemony of liberalism, liberal institutions were a kind of protective coloration, helping to legitimate a Latin American government in the eyes of the metropolitan powers.

Third, insofar as the masses themselves became politically aware (as, for example, the middle and working classes in Argentina did in the late nineteenth century), their participation in elections and other liberal institutions served to legitimate the system in the eyes of the people themselves. This of course is a mechanism we have already taken note of when we examined the emergence of liberal democracy in the North Atlantic countries.

To summarize, in the industrializing countries of the North Atlantic during the nineteenth century liberalism became the dominant force shaping economy and polity, as well as modes of thinking. In the political realm this meant the emergence of essentially liberal states which increasingly were legitimated through such democratic institutions as universal suffrage. In the dependent countries of Latin America, by contrast, states remained essentially centralist, but they were increasingly legitimated through liberal and even democratic institutions. In the North Atlantic liberalism was real and democracy symbolic; in Latin America both liberalism and democracy were symbolic.

## Liberal Democracy in Latin America: A Twentieth-Century Overview

If Latin America is simply not very hospitable to liberal democracy, if the variables which usually accompany it elsewhere are of little help in explaining its presence or absence in Latin America, then how do we explain, how may we come to understand, the deviant cases, the few sustained examples of liberal democracy.

If we use the rather conventional definition of liberal democracy stipulated near the beginning of this chapter (that is, emphasizing universal suffrage, free and competitive elections, and freedom of organization and political action) and if we add the stipulation that such a regime be maintained for some significant length of time (say, fifteen years), then we have a working definition of stable liberal democracy. Given these criteria, it will not be difficult for students of Latin America to agree on the following propositions:

1. No such regime existed in Latin America prior to 1900.
2. Suffrage did not approach universality until the adoption of female suffrage, after World War II almost everywhere.
3. After World War II stable liberal democracies took root in Chile, Uruguay, and Costa Rica; later came Venezuela and the highly problematical case of Colombia.
4. In all these cases save Venezuela, the way was prepared for liberal democracy by prolonged periods of "proto-democracy," in which competing elites sought office through elections, left office when they lost elections, and respected a wide range of citizen political liberties; Argentina (and perhaps Peru) also

saw substantial periods of proto-democracy, but in those cases stable liberal democracies did not follow.

A brief summary of the twentieth-century career of democracy in each of these countries will clarify the picture (Wiarda and Kline, eds., 1979). In every case of sustained liberal democracy the regime has been founded on some form of explicit accommodation between rival elites, guaranteeing that the capture of control of the government by any of them, through honest elections, would not threaten the vital interests of the losers or permanently exclude them from power. In some ways, Chile is an exception to this generalization, since its stability from the 1930s to 1970 seems to have been based not on elite accommodation but on mutual acceptance of a constitutional framework characterized by numerous checks and balances that served to prevent any group from monopolizing power. In the cases in which sustained democratic regimes were not established, neither elite accommodation nor commitment to a constitution protected the democratic regime from partisan conflict (for a fuller elaboration of this argument, see Peeler, 1983).

In Argentina a tightly restricted civil oligarchy dominated by the great landowners was challenged by the urban, middle-class-based Radical Civic Union after the 1890s. The most important demand of the Radicals was precisely the democratization of the political system through expansion of the suffrage and elimination of corruption. The Sáenz Peña Law, enacted in 1912 by the Conservatives, was an attempt to co-opt the Radicals by granting their key demands while leaving the Conservatives in charge. But that was a miscalculation: the Radicals used the new law to elect Hipólito Yrigoyen as president in 1916. Yrigoyen and another, antagonistic Radical faction alternated in power until 1930, when the armed forces staged a reactionary coup on behalf of the old ruling class and largely reversed the democratization. This reactionary civil-military alliance lasted until 1943, when it was deposed by a coup of pro-Axis, nationalistic junior officers, including Col. Juan Perón. Perón used his position as minister of labor to build a clientele among the working class, never before politically mobilized in Argentina. With the Allied victory, Perón deemphasized his proto-fascism in favor of a worker-oriented populism (with the support and encouragement of his second wife, Evita) and established a supremacy that lasted until the economy turned sour in the early 1950s.

After his overthrow in 1955 a succession of military regimes alternated with brief elected governments, none of which lasted through its mandate. Perón had left behind an organized movement based in the labor unions, which persistently demanded his return. The armed forces just as persistently refused to permit that. The result was prolonged political impasse from 1955 until 1973. In that year the military government finally admitted that repression had not worked and that Argentina's political problems could not be solved without the Peronists. After free elections, Perón again became president. His supporters quickly split into left and right wings, however, the former demanding a socialist revolution. After less than a year, Perón's ineffectual presidency ended with his death. His wife and vice president, Isabel, succeeded him and came increasingly under the influence of extreme right-wing ideologues. Her support eroding and the national economy in a disastrous slide, she was overthrown by the armed forces in 1976 and replaced by yet another military regime dedicated to conservative economic policy and the violent depoliticization of Argentine society. The defeat in the Malvinas in 1982 forced the retirement of the military president, Galtieri, and led in 1983 to another civilian regime, but it is uncertain whether the leadership and cohesion that would be necessary to a stable democracy will emerge.

Chile also was dominated after the 1890s by a conservative civilian regime representing landholding interests. The Chilean Radicals also emerged from a middle-class base to challenge the power monopoly and were the key to the election of Arturo Alessandri as president in 1920. The period from the late 1920s into the early 1930s was marked by prolonged instability as political forces from conservative to socialist struggled to define the regime. The key break with the course Argentina followed came in 1938, when a center-left popular front of Radicals, Socialists, and Communists won the presidential election—and were allowed to take office and complete the term. This allowed for broadening the effective electorate and the acceptable political spectrum while maintaining liberal political institutions. This was the beginning of Chilean liberal democracy (though suffrage continued to be restricted by literacy requirements until 1970). From 1938 through 1973 Chile had numerous free elections and a vigorous multiparty system with the Radicals at its center until they were supplanted by the Christian Democrats in the 1960s. But the victory of a Socialist-Communist coalition (Unidad Popular) in the presidential elections of 1970 and subsequent efforts to secure a fundamental redistribution of resources stretched Chilean liberal democracy to the breaking point. In 1973, after nearly three years of economic turmoil and political conflict, the armed forces seized power and imposed a stringently repressive regime dedicated to laissez-faire economics and political demobilization of the population. After a decade of political repression and rigidly free-market economic policies, Chile was particularly hard hit by the worldwide economic crisis, touching off protests that quickly escalated into demands for the resignation of General Pinochet and immediate democratic elections. At this writing, the days of the regime seem to be numbered, but the future is uncertain.

Colombia entered the twentieth century through the fiery baptism of the War of a Thousand Days, a destructive civil war between armies of Liberals and Conservatives which was an unsuccessful attempt on the part of the former to break the hegemony of the latter in the national government. The political system was at that time the preserve of a small elite based on coffee and trade and divided by traditional Liberal and Conservative party loyalties. Although political participation was the prerogative of the elite, large parts of the population were tied to one or the other party by means of patron-client ties, which made them available for either voting or fighting, depending on the circumstance. When a party held control of the presidency, as the Conservatives did at the turn of the century, its leaders used it to establish national hegemony by controlling elections and ousting opposing partisans from patronage positions throughout the country. The opposition party, however, always retained some local and regional bases of power, and usually some representation in Congress. The rival parties shared an awareness that, as the country's dominant elite, they had mutual interests. Often bipartisan coalitions were formed to heal wounds resulting from civil war or the transfer of the government from one party's control to that of the other.

This dynamically stable elite republic began to come unraveled in the 1930s. The Liberals captured the presidency in the election of 1930, taking advantage of a split in the Conservative party. In 1934, Liberal Alfonso López Pumarejo was elected, and he began a process of political and economic reforms that expanded the suffrage and created the beginnings of a welfare state. Not surprisingly, most of the new voters turned out to be Liberals. A populist Liberal, Jorge Eliécer Gaitán, emerged to the left of López to build a large following among the urban masses. The Conservatives of course could see that the possibilities of their recapturing power were receding; their response came in the militantly reactionary agitation of Laureano Gómez, who increasingly lumped Liberals with Communists as alien to the Colombian way of life, deserving of repression if not extermination. The Conservatives were able to recapture the national government in 1946, when the Liberals split between the *gaitanista* and moderate wings. The process of purging Liberals from positions of power assumed unusual violence and provoked resistance. Gaitán, who had gained control of the Liberal party and seemed certain to win the 1950 elections, was assassinated in Bogotá in April 1948, touching off massive urban riots and feeding the continuing violence in the countryside. Thousands of people were killed in the rural violence, which began as partisan and official repression of Liberals and Liberal resistance. Gradually, though, the violence assumed its own dynamic, with components of blood vengeance, simple crime, organized crime, and revolutionary insurgency on top of the original partisan conflict. By 1953 most leaders of both parties had come to see that their very control of the society was threatened; most of both parties supported the coup of Gen. Rojas Pinilla in hopes that a temporary nonpartisan government could break the cycle of violence. Although he made some headway, Rojas was not totally successful, and when he began building an independent political base for permanent replacement of the parties, their leaderships combined to have the armed forces remove him in 1957.

The following year the National Front was initiated. The Front was a constitutionally sanctioned grand coalition in which the presidency would alternate between Liberals and Conservatives for sixteen years, while other elective and appointive offices would be divided evenly between the parties. The manifest purpose was to eliminate the main reason for partisan conflict—patronage—and to reduce the level of excitement in the political arena in order to demobilize the population politically. The party elites were trying to put the genie of mass political participation back in the bottle before it consumed them. It worked (though possibly only fraud prevented Rojas from winning the presidency in 1970). The National Front ended in 1974, and has been replaced by a more open liberal democracy. The system is still completely dominated by the traditional parties, with low levels of mass participation. The Liberals won the presidency in 1974 and 1978; the Conservatives used a Liberal split to win in 1982. What consequences the Conservative victory may have are still unclear.

Costa Rican politics at the turn of the century were also

the preserve of the small elite, again largely based on coffee and trade, but without the highly institutionalized parties, political conflict centered on personalities. In fact, the informal but dominant organizing principle of politics was personal hegemony: from the presidency a man could exert sufficient control over patronage and other benefits to dominate the whole political process even after the end of his term. Such a hegemony took a very mild form in Costa Rica: violence was rare, opposition was always present, and the leader did not always get his way. But the political process was still clearly dominated by an identifiable person most of the time.

The 1940s mark the end of this elitist republic. Rafael Angel Calderón Guardia was elected president in 1940. Attempting to secure his own hegemony by appealing to and mobilizing the working class, he sponsored a new labor law and created a social security system. Conservative propertied interests reacted with hostility to these political and economic innovations. Encouraged by the Allied war effort of World War II, Calderón turned to the Communists for support in the face of militant conservative opposition; that of course intensified conservative hostility. An emerging social democratic movement opposed Calderón as well. They too were hostile to Communist participation in the government, and they strongly condemned the corruption that was rampant in the Calderón government and its calderonista successor. A disputed presidential election in 1948 led to a civil war in which Calderón was defeated.

A junta headed by Social Democrat José Figueres was installed. In a year in power, the junta nationalized the banks and dissolved the army, while it maintained the social gains enacted under Calderón. The calderonistas and Communists, however, were outlawed, and the conservative groups humiliated the Social Democrats in elections for a constituent assembly, obliging them to accept a much more conservative constitution than they had wished. In 1949, Figueres handed over power to Otilio Ulate, victor in the

1948 elections, and turned his attention to organizing a more effective party, the Partido Liberación Nacional (PLN), which swept him to victory in the presidential elections of 1953. Thereafter, PLN administrations alternated with shifting coalitions of anti-PLN conservative forces (except for 1970 and 1974, when the PLN won consecutively). The Costa Rican democracy has remained procedurally flawed by prolonged efforts to outlaw the Communist party and by the retention of a literacy requirement for voting (mitigated by a literacy rate of over 90 percent). The regime has been stable, though seemingly unable to generate structural reforms. Its stability is currently threatened by a prolonged economic crisis.

Like the other countries discussed, Peru was controlled by a small civilian elite in the early twentieth century, an elite based on agriculture, mining, and trade. The mass of the rural population, mostly Indian, was completely outside the political system, save for the physical labor it provided to sustain the society. But the emergence of an urban, mining, and petroleum working class, as well as an urban middle class, provided the basis for a populist reformist movement called APRA (Alianza Popular Revolucionario Americano), led by Víctor Raúl Haya de la Torre. By the late 1920s the militant APRA was widely seen as a serious threat to take power in Peru. That touched off the first of many coups which acted as military vetoes on the accession of APRA to power. From the 1930s until 1968 Peruvian politics alternated between military regimes allied with Peru's propertied interests and civilian regimes equally close to those interests, but existing under the shadow of military intervention should APRA ever seem close to winning an election. During this period, APRA itself became steadily more conservative and more opportunistic in its pursuit of power, but this did not mollify the armed forces.

Finally, in 1968 a unique military coup took place, which brought to power a military regime committed to egalitarian, structural social reforms. In addition to petroleum nationalization, which provided the occasion for the coup, the regime sponsored the most extensive agrarian reform in Peruvian history and promoted experiments in participatory self-government and community development in poor urban and rural areas. After eight years, however, Peru's dependent capitalist economy thoroughly disrupted, the impetus for reform was exhausted, and a more conservative junta took over. Before the end of the decade, a constituent assembly had been elected, a constitution adopted, free elections held, and (with Haya de la Torre dead and APRA split) a new president and congress elected (Fernando Belaúnde, the president overthrown in 1968, was returned to power). Today, troubled by a world recession and a resurgence of terrorism, the Belaúnde administration may not last out its term.

Venezuela entered the twentieth century with a political system and social structure strikingly different from those of the other countries discussed here. With an economy based on coffee and cattle, political power had been held by a series of regionally based caudillos in alliance with commercial interests in Caracas. At the turn of the century a new ruling group had just conquered power; this group came from the Andean states and drew its economic base from coffee. In 1908, Cipriano Castro was overthrown by his fellow Andean Juan Vicente Gómez, who was to rule until his death in 1935. He was a virtuoso caudillo, and in his assiduous and successful efforts to stay in power, he made it impossible for another traditional caudillo ever again to arise in Venezuela.

Like any caudillo, he treated the country as his own private ranch, but he transformed Venezuela into a modern nation. To make his armed forces well disciplined and loyal, and to assure that they would be able to defeat any internal rival, he insisted that they be professionalized. Authorizing exploitation of petroleum, he used the royalties to enhance the capabilities of his government and to promote development of the society through road-building and other construction and through an expansion of education. He promoted all these changes because he expected to be able to rake off more benefits for himself and his friends and relatives (as indeed he did). He never intended to lose control of this rapidly changing society (as indeed he had not at his death), but he had no way of understanding the depths of the changes that were occurring, fueled by petroleum. The forty years after the death of Gómez may now be seen as a convulsive rearrangement of almost everything about the society to make it more congruent with the new reality of petroleum. The transformation is certainly not over yet.

Politically, a decade of cautious, controlled liberalization by the heirs of Gómez was cut short in 1945 by a civil-military coup led by the reformist party Acción Democrática (AD). There followed a three-year attempt to push through a social democratic revolution, but the party's power base was inadequate without control over the military and without allies in the most important economic sectors. Another coup by the original military coconspirators overthrew the AD regime in 1948. Nine years of military corruption and repression taught AD, its party rivals, and the business community the value of accommodation to one another's interests. The military regime was overthrown in January 1958, and free elections were held in December of that year.

AD was again victorious, but unlike its previous tenure, the leadership made special efforts to avoid threatening the vital interests of other parties and the business community. The latter groups in turn collaborated with, rather than conspire against, the AD government. The price of this accommodation was the breakaway of AD's left wing and its collaboration with the Communists in an insurgency which raged in the early to middle 1960s before it was finally defeated. The 1968 election victory of the opposition Christian Democratic party, COPEI, the successful amnesty of the former guerrillas and their integration into electoral politics in the 1973 election, and, finally, the definitive emergence of two-party (AD-COPEI) dominance in the elections of 1973 and 1978 were the elements of the stabilized liberal democratic regime that emerged after 1973. The AD victory in the 1983 elections confirmed this pattern.

After the turn of the century Uruguay moved more quickly than any of the other countries mentioned to break with its traditional, elite-based two-party competition between Blancos and Colorados. The election of José Batlle as president led to major democratizing reforms and the initiation of the Uruguayan welfare state. Then Batlle successfully promoted a constitutional reform setting up a plural executive with assured representation for the minority party in the plural executive itself and in the cabinet.

Yet if most of the reforms were left intact in subsequent decades, their nationalistic spirit and intellectual integrity were lost. Batlle had been convinced that Uruguay must and could industrialize using its own capital resources, and that it was proper for the government, with a concern for the common interest, to lead that development. The governments that succeeded Batlle, from 1916 on, tended to see in the reforms simply a source of jobs; the bureaucracy tended inexorably to expand, with remarkably little concern or effort directed toward paying the costs of these programs. Batlle sought to move the country toward the establishment of self-sustaining industrial growth, but very little progress was made to that end after 1916. The country remained totally dependent on the exports of an agricultural economy that was permitted slowly to sink into decrepitude.

A political system premised on shared power for all established interests, on patronage rather than policy coherence, could discuss these issues at great length, but was not equipped to resolve them. Instead, when the nation's problems periodically reached crisis proportions, the usual response was to release pressure by changing the organization of the government, from collegial, to presidential, and back. Thus in the context of the world economic crisis of the 1930s, President Gabriel Terra, a Colorado, collaborated with sectors of the Blancos to reestablish a presidential constitution. Terra was in effect a dictator for ten years, but the presidential constitution persisted for another decade. In 1951, a resurgence of radical *batllismo* led by Luis Batlle Berres, a nephew of the older Batlle, led more conservative sectors of the Colorados (including the sons of Batlle y Ordóñez) to cooperate with the Blancos in pushing through a reestablishment of the plural executive, probably as a means of keeping Batlle Berres in check. Finally, the apparently irreversible and accelerating economic slide of the late 1950s and 1960s led to the reestablishment of a presidential constitution in 1966.

In the 1950s and 1960s the economy stagnated and the state descended into a deepening fiscal crisis. A violent left opposition emerged with the Tupamaros in the late 1960s, provoking the progressive militarization of the state and leading to the de facto seizure of power in 1973. That military regime proved as repressive and economically conservative as its neighbors in Argentina and Chile. At the end of the decade, seeking controlled civilianization, the regime staged a referendum on its proposed new constitution. The resounding no vote advertised the stupidity of the leadership and certainly shook its confidence. A return to civilian liberal democracy seems well within the range of possibility within the next few years.

## Theories of Democracy in the Latin American Context

Even though some of these countries have developed liberal democracies that can meet—or very nearly meet—the same criteria as those of the North Atlantic area, the explanations that are useful for the northern democracies are not very fruitful in Latin America. Phillip Coulter found that relationships between social mobilization and liberal democracy, which are strong on a global level, are weak in Latin America. The class analysis of Moore is of little help be cause the class structures of the countries in question differ profoundly from one another, and all are radically distinct from anything found in Western Europe. Nevertheless, Moore's insistence on the centrality of class structure is methodologically instructive. The Latin American cases in the Linz-Stepan volume and in Gabriel Almond, Scott Flanagan, and Robert Mundt's *Crisis, Choice, and Change* call attention to the relative autonomy of actors in crisis situations in determining the future course of political systems. But though this approach is a useful corrective, it cannot eliminate the need to understand structural constraints that no individual can change.

Studies that start with a specific focus on Latin America have been more successful in developing plausible understandings of democracy in the region. Samuel P. Huntington's classic study *Political Order in Changing Societies* (1968) played a crucial role in breaking the notion that the emergence of modernization in traditional societies would, as a matter of course, lead also to stable, liberal democracy. Quite the contrary, Huntington argued, the massive social changes entailed by modernization would tend to undermine the stability of existing political orders (which would be unable to cope with the changes), but without necessarily generating more modern and capable institutions. As the social mobilization accompanying modernization outruns the capabilities of political institutions to control the society, what emerges is a chronically unstable, "praetorian" regime in which the seizure of power by force is frequent. Huntington uses Argentina as an example of a praetorian society at very high levels of social mobilization, in which the armed forces seize power in order to prevent a highly organized and self-conscious working class from gaining control of the government. The prescription Huntington derives from this structural imbalance calls for increasing the capacity of government to control the society and, if possible, the political demobilization of the population (pp. 85–86). This was in fact the strategy adopted by military regimes in Brazil, Argentina, Uruguay, and Chile in the late 1960s and early 1970s.

Guillermo O'Donnell (1979) took note of this a few years later in setting forth his very influential theory of the "bureaucratic-authoritarian regime" in Latin America. While Huntington explained these peculiarly ideological and repressive military regimes simply as attempts to reassert control over a rapidly changing society, O'Donnell went further by specifying an economic context: the exhaustion of import substitution as a strategy of economic development. As Latin American societies reached the point at which further economic growth depended on depressing wages and working conditions, O'Donnell argued, the coercive power of a military regime was necessary. A liberal democratic regime would be highly unlikely to survive such a major, structural economic crisis.

Looking at the same resurgence of authoritarian regimes in the 1960s and 1970s, Howard Wiarda chose to emphasize neither political nor economic factors, but rather the Iberian cultural resistance to liberal values, including those of liberal democracy (1980). In an argument basically consistent with that of Véliz (1980), cited earlier in this chapter, Wiarda simply holds that authoritarian, corporatist leadership is most natural in the Latin American cultural sphere. In fact, he advocates a reconceptualization of democracy and human rights for the Latin American context. And while the notion of redefining these terms to fit Latin American standards may just lead to terminological confusion, Wiarda's attempt to define the limits of a government's exercise of legitimate authority is quite perceptive and useful. Observe, for example, his analysis of representation and participation as expectations of government in Latin America:

> Government must be both "representative" and
> "participatory," but in the Latin American sense of
> those terms. It must be representative of "society,"
> meaning those groups (church, army, labor, elites, etc.)

that have been duly recognized by the state and given official sanction as legitimate "power contenders" in the system. These groups are usually represented in the cabinet, congress, or council of state, through the ministries of state agencies, and with special access to the centers of decision making. The state must also provide for "participation" through a generally officially sanctioned network of associations for workers, farmers, women, and so forth. To the extent it allows such "representation" and "participation," a government may be considered "democratic"; but to the degree it closes off or stifles such legitimate group life, it may lose its democratic standing. Note, however, that not all elements are represented in this scheme (e.g., unorganized peasants, Indians, or urban marginals), nor is the principle of one man/one vote necessarily applicable. (Pp. 245–46.)

A highly provocative examination of democracy in Latin America was published in 1979 by Göran Therborn. He uses a particularly narrow and formal definition of democracy which has the puzzling effect of excluding both Chile and Costa Rica as full democracies, while including Colombia in that category. But while Therborn's treatment of individual countries is superficial and often questionable, his overall perspective on the problem is amply deserving of examination. After arguing that Latin American experiments with democracy have resulted from the complex interaction of international circumstances with local conditions of class struggle, Therborn notes that in no case was a firm basis laid for stable democracy (or for capitalist development).

He further argues that the reason democracies have been so rare and so unstable in Latin America is that, in contrast to Europe, the formation of a stable bourgeois state has never been accomplished. In Western Europe the state was well established before the struggle for democratization began. The explanation for the weakness of Latin American states lies in their international economic situation. Since colonial times they have been dominated economically (external control of basic resources and means of production), politically (external penetration of the territory by another state), and ideologically (massive importation of external ideas and external control of ideological apparatuses such as education). Moreover, their relation to the international capitalist system has been one of incorporation rather than integration:

> *Integration* would then refer to cases of all pervasive and complete penetration and transformation, to the point where the parts of the local system are all interconnected by means of capitalist and commodity relations which represent only a territorially-bounded segment of the world system. *Incorporation*, on the other hand, would mean that the local system is linked with—and dependent upon—the international system, while not being pervaded by it. The local unit is, so to speak, swallowed but not digested by the system. Or put the other way round, the local unit has not been able fully to digest the system or transform it into energy of its own. Instead there remain internal disarticulations, due both to the absence of organic links between the various capitalist sectors, and to the coexistence of these sectors with non-capitalist, non-commodity relations. (P. 100.)

This dominated and incorporated position in the international capitalist system undermines the unity, stability, and power of the state and also discourages cohesion in the bourgeoisie, the working class, and the peasantry. With a weak state and a disunited bourgeoisie, any kind of stable regime is impossible. Without cohesive subordinate classes, there will be no effective pressure for democratization. Therborn suggests that the exceptions "when there have been long periods of stable non-despotic rule" (for example, in Brazil, Chile, Costa Rica, Mexico, or Uruguay) can be explained by the presence of local conditions that compensate for the inherent tendencies of dominated incorporation. Central among such local conditions would be a relative unity of the local bourgeoisie. Similarly, a bourgeoisie may be expected to take unified and effective action against a dictatorship and in favor of democratization only if capitalism itself is not threatened and if the dictatorship lacks an organic base in some sectors of the bourgeoisie.

## Conclusion

The idea of democracy has been a widespread one in Latin America, and in a form not too dissimilar from the theory of liberal democracy as developed in the industrial societies of the North Atlantic. Most Latin American experiments with liberal democracy, however, have been brief and unstable. In attempting to explain why some such democracies have proven more durable than others, we have found no single theoretical model very promising.

The following chapters will examine in detail the surviving, relatively stable democratic regimes in Colombia, Costa Rica, and Venezuela in order to shed further light on the problem. We will see that it is difficult to discern major common features in the process of evolution of democratic regimes in these three countries, but easier to see similarities in the three regimes once established. Democratization in all three cases seems to have been built on a period of elite competition for political power, a competition sufficiently muted by accommodation to keep it within the bounds of civility most of the time. Democratization was in each case demanded by emerging mass-based political movements which were able in due course to extract enough concessions from the dominant elites to establish a formally liberal democracy. The stability of the liberal democracy, though, depended on the willingness of the democratizing reformers to accommodate elite interests by for-going major structural changes in economy and society. The liberal democratic regimes in the three countries are thus characterized by a self-conscious accommodation of elites, and policy consensus on a mixed capitalist economy and ameliorative rather than structurally radical social reforms. Liberal democratic electoral institutions and political pro-cesses enhance the legitimacy of the regime by assuring broad access, while effectively making marginal any ex-treme opposition from the left or right. Finally, both the emergence and the maintenance of these regimes have been significantly affected by international economic and politi-cal conditions.

# 2

*The Emergence of*
*Liberal Democracy*
*in Latin America:*
*Three Paths*

## *Introduction*

Although Colombia, Costa Rica, and Venezuela obviously share a great many characteristics and experiences beyond the fact of being liberal democracies, it is quite difficult in comparing their historical development to discern common roots of modern liberal democracy. Costa Rica has had a multiparty democracy with frequent opposition electoral victories since 1953, and Venezuela since 1959. From 1958 to 1974 Colombia had honest elections (excepting, possibly, 1970) within the National Front framework, which controlled interparty competition. Since 1974 the system has moved much closer to liberal democratic standards: in 1982 the Conservatives won the presidency over the incumbent Liberals in a freely contested and honestly counted election.

The common elements of their experiences do not help us much: all were colonized by the Spanish, became Catholic societies, and had coffee as the first major export crop reliable over a long period, which promoted economic dependence and financed infrastructural development and social change. Other countries that have not become liberal democracies have of course also shared these characteristics, so they cannot in themselves be seen as crucial factors. Directly political characteristics are more useful in explaining the emergence of liberal democracy: the three governments under study all underwent a predemocratic period of civil elite competition and controlled expansion of political participation, which included conscious and explicit accommodation between rival elites. Still, the dominant message of this chapter has to be that there is no single road to liberal democracy in Latin America (compare the recent study by Wesson, 1982).

# Colombia: Controlled Democratization of a Traditional Party System

Bogotá in the eighteenth century had been the seat of the Viceroyalty of Nueva Granada, which included present-day Colombia and Panama and the outlying provinces of Quito (that is, Ecuador) and Venezuela.[1] The area of present-day Colombia entered the nineteenth century with several centers of modest economic prosperity in mining, textiles, and agriculture, which produced both for export and for internal consumption. This economic base had promoted the development of regionally distributed creole economic and social elites who held most of the land, mines, and mills and who predominated in trade and the learned professions. Of course, there were Spanish officials as well—civil, military, and ecclesiastical. As elsewhere in South America, rivalry between the creole elites and the officials was a major source of the tension that led to the independence movement. But the elites also had to be concerned with controlling popular discontent, which broke into serious challenges to authority on numerous occasions, such as the 1782 Comuneros rebellion against Spanish taxation (see Phelan, 1978); their grievances notwithstanding, therefore, the creole elites would not lightly undermine colonial authority.

The bulk of the population, exploited by the elites, lived on the land as laborers, sharecroppers, or owners of tiny plots of land (minifundistas). Most of these people were Spanish-speaking mestizos; few Indians still cultivated communal lands. Near the Caribbean coast African slaves had been brought in. Laborers and artisans were significant in the cities, in industrial centers such as Socorro (textiles), and in the mining areas (especially around Antioquia and Popayán).

It is important to remember that the lives of these common people—even those with property—did not resemble that of a North American pioneer or small farmer, who was relatively independent. They lived in a hierarchical society in which they were near or at the bottom, and securing aid or clemency from those above them economically or politically was a daily necessity. The issue might involve the right to a plot of land, a loan to buy seeds or pay taxes, the need for patronage on one's business, or any of a number of other obligations. In any of these situations one needed help and protection from someone with more power. The patron-client relationship was a basic building block of colonial society: the client offered support, obedience, and loyalty in the tacit expectation of the patron's protection (Schmidt, 1974a, b, c, 1980).

When Spanish control of America began to unravel under the impact of the Napoleonic conquests, the creole elites of Nueva Granada and elsewhere were concerned to seize political command of the territory without endangering the clientelistic authority structure from which they benefited. And on the whole they were successful. The independence movement of Nueva Granada emerged in response to and in collaboration with the somewhat earlier movement of Venezuelan creoles led by Simón Bolívar. Although there was a great deal of fighting in Nueva Granada and the population, both elite and mass, was profoundly divided by the struggle, the basic social structure survived the struggle intact (in striking contrast to Venezuela). To put it very simply, those with property retained the ability to dominate those without it, even though the propertied had paid a heavy price for independence.

Freed of the restraining hand of Spain, what the new rulers of Nueva Granada would do with their dominance was a major political issue. The sociopolitical system they inherited was distinctly bureaucratic, legalistic, centralized, and unliberal. This colonial order both supported and drew legitimation from the Roman Catholic church, whose teachings emphasized submission to established authority and suppression of unorthodox thought. Those who opposed the colonial authorities found little inspiration in the Hispanic tradition itself; thus, they drew on the liberal doctrines of the Enlightenment and the American and French revolutions for ideological support. In Nueva Granada, as elsewhere, the rhetoric and the constitutions of the independence era were replete with such liberal ideas as individual and collective rights of self-determination and freedom of religion.

These liberal ideas, however, not only were ill suited to the clientelistic structure of political power but also directly challenged the interests of the church and all those who would benefit from continuation of a centralized and authoritarian political and economic order. These three elements—liberalism, clientelism, and centralism—interacted in complex ways to shape the political economy of Colombia.

Virtually the entire country was organized on the basis of patron-client relationships between a property owner and his dependents and employees. The wealthier and more prominent families frequently held diverse interests in agriculture, domestic and international commerce, mining, and manufacturing. Everyone who depended on one of these enterprises for a living would be expected, among other obligations, to support the patron's political interests, even by bearing arms if asked to do so. To wield national power, including placing an ally in the presidency, patrons would have to build national alliances capable of controlling large numbers of votes or, if necessary, arms. In part, then, parties emerged in Colombia, as elsewhere, as rival coalitions seeking control of political institutions.

The parties did have doctrinal differences, though not so profound in practice as in rhetoric. The Conservatives placed great emphasis on reaffirming traditional Hispanic values, including most notably the central and privileged position of the church; they feared the subversion of the old hierarchical social order of colonial times by the secular values of the new industrial age. Liberals tended to favor a more secular order, with restrictions on the role and power of the church. Conservatives tended to be centralists, and

Liberals federalists. Over a broad range of important policy issues, however, the leaders of the two parties differed hardly at all. Both parties accepted the liberal notion of constitutional and republican government as a norm, while Liberals and Conservatives alike clung to the clientelist practices that negated the liberal notion of free and equal citizenship. Both were in favor of classical liberal economic policies: from the emergence of Nueva Granada as an independent state in 1830 until the 1890s, Liberal and Conservative governments pursued a policy of free trade which progressively integrated Colombia into the international economy as a producer of raw materials and agricultural products, while destroying what nascent manufacturing had existed at the time of independence.

This substantial coincidence of views reflects the similar social composition of the parties: each distinctly polyclass, each led by a coalition of propertied individuals and families with diversified interests. They might disagree on cultural issues and they might do battle for control of the government, but the Colombian ruling class was virtually unanimous in favoring free trade, opening up the country in order to reach European markets with competitively priced raw materials and to use the proceeds to buy European manufactured goods of better quality and lower price than those made in Colombia. The disastrous effect of this practice on such artisans as the textile producers of Socorro was scarcely lamented in Colombian ruling circles. When organized artisans combined with underpaid and disgruntled army officers to try to seize power in 1854, Liberal and Conservative leaders stood together, mobilizing their armed clienteles to put down one of the rare class-based challenges to the Colombian ruling order (Guillén Martínez, 1979, chap. 8).

This bipartisan coalition gave way to the militantly Conservative presidency of Mariano Ospina Rodríguez in 1857, after the only direct, male-suffrage presidential election of the century. Ospina could antagonize the Liberals in their regional power bases, but he could not subdue them. The

Federal War broke out in early 1860 and lasted until 1863, one of the bloodiest civil wars of the century. The ultimate victors were the Liberals, and they reaffirmed their commitment to decentralized, federal government, a constitutional framework that would last more than twenty years.

This period of hyperliberalism, a reflection of the great power of Liberal regional chiefs who would not submit to central control, failed to promote the economic growth that seemed to be promised by the free trade gospel. The economy as a whole had been essentially stagnant since independence, though there had been small and short-lived centers of prosperity.[2] One such boomlet involved production and export of tobacco, but it never achieved great national impact, and the industry decayed in the 1870s. Another major export crop, coffee, began to be exploited on a major scale around mid-century in Santander (adjacent to Venezuela, where cultivation had started somewhat earlier). Coffee would provide the base for economic growth in Colombia.

But coffee cultivation on a grand scale could not develop as long as Colombia was racked by instability and warfare and the government was unable to carry through construction of the essential infrastructure. By the 1880s growing sectors of the Liberal leadership had become convinced that no matter how open Colombia's trade policy might be, it had to have a government capable of maintaining order and promoting development. Much of the Colombian ruling class united behind dissident Liberal Rafael Núñez, who was able to capture the presidency in coalition with the Conservatives. This coalition persisted for a few years and then gave way to a Conservative political hegemony that would persist until 1930.

Núñez's rise coincided with that of coffee; the main area of cultivation shifted to Antioquia and adjacent central Colombia, where production rapidly expanded. Infrastructural development and the stabilization of banking and commerce assisted the development of coffee production. An economic structure in Antioquia characterized by dispersed (though still highly unequal) landownership had several positive consequences. The large numbers of smallholdings on broken terrain were well suited to labor-intensive, high-value coffee production, and the modest increase in purchasing power which coffee yielded to these farmers provided a consumer market for the first successful Colombian industries in the early twentieth century. At the same time, a much smaller number of large growers, processors, and exporters were able to accumulate capital for investment in manufacturing, commerce, and banking, as well as back into agriculture. By the early twentieth century coffee had become the linchpin of the Colombian economy.

The transition of 1886 suggests that Colombia had developed a political cycle like those of other Latin American countries (see Table 1). In Costa Rica and Venezuela, and elsewhere in Latin America in the nineteenth century, an individual often gained control of the national government through the arms of a supporting coalition of allied patrons and their clients. He would then place supporters in all significant positions of power or patronage, from which vantage points they could control violent resistance and determine the outcome of elections. Then a docile constituent assembly could be elected to draft a new constitution along lines desired by the new leader. The leader could then assure an alternation in the presidency between himself and his supporters, until such time as disgruntled supporters might coalesce with opposition elements to overthrow him.

The peculiarity of Colombian politics is that personal, patrimonial rule was transmuted into party hegemony. In Colombia after the later 1840s parties that originated in clientelistic coalitions for the conquest of power became institutionalized to the point that they persisted over generations, surviving the rise and fall of individual leaders and the loss of power by the party itself. Both elites and the mass of the population came to be associated with one party or the other, their commitments fed by regular partisan elections, by the resentments left over from periodic wars, and

TABLE I
*Periods of Party Hegemony in Colombia*

| Hegemonic Party | Approximate Dates | Transitional Periods |
| --- | --- | --- |
| | | 1850–63 |
| Liberal | 1863–86 | |
| | | 1886–90 |
| Conservative | 1890–1930 | |
| | | 1930–34 |
| Liberal | 1934–46 | |
| | | 1946–48 |
| Conservative | 1948–53 | |
| | | 1953–57 |

by the knowledge that the direct and indirect benefits of patronage would be lost if the other side won.

Since the parties were so stable, the unraveling and death of a government did not lead to the destruction of its party, even if its partisans lost national power. They retained many local power bases, which the triumphant opposition could not easily eliminate because of the strength of clientelistic ties. Moreover, the regional chiefs retained alliances between themselves which could be used for defense and for preparing a return to power.

The parties were conscious of their permanence and their joint ownership of the political system. They evolved a distinctive transitional device, the bipartisan coalition, composed of the former opposition party and dissident elements of the displaced governing party. Such coalitions broadened the base of the new government in order to assure stability; they typically gave way to a single-party hegemony after a year or two. Coalitions were formed in 1854 (leading to Ospina's Conservative government), 1886 (under Núñez's auspices, leading to a Conservative hegemony), 1903 (under Rafael Reyes in the wake of the War of a Thousand Days, this coalition reinforced the Conservative victory, 1930 (leading to a Liberal hegemony), and 1945–46 (leading to a Conservative hegemony). The National Front of 1958–74 was only the latest, longest lasting, and most formal of many bipartisan coalitions.

The predemocratic party system went through a maturing or stabilization process prior to the presidency of Alfonso López in 1934. From the formation of the parties in the late 1840s until Núñez's capture of the presidency in 1886, both parties were quite militant in pushing policies that were anathema to the opposition, and indeed in seeking to destroy the opposition party as a political force. This militance can be seen not only in the Federal War (1860–63) itself but also in the partisan and doctrinaire presidencies of Jose Hilario López (Liberal) and Mariano Ospina Rodríguez (Conservative) and the series of Liberal federal governments after the war. Only in response to the artisans' revolt of 1854 did the leaderships of the two parties briefly suspend their rivalry to secure their joint interest in keeping the common people under control.

By contrast, after 1886 there was a distinct mellowing of partisan spirit. The Conservatives, then in control, reaffirmed the privileged role of the church, but placed much more emphasis on economic development and political stability. They did not seriously attempt to root out Liberal redoubts of local power. The Liberals, in turn, finally accepted the establishment of the church and its substantial role in secular affairs. After one more massive Liberal insurrection (the War of a Thousand Days, 1899–1902) and the ensuing loss of Panama, a spirit of considerable partisan accommodation characterized the first third of the twentieth century, within the framework of Conservative dominance. The calm was marred only by a rash of bitter strikes marking the beginning of labor organization and by the populist agitation of the Liberal war hero Rafael Uribe Uribe (until his assassination in 1914).

Though easily contained by the regime, these agitations were indications of changes taking place in Colombian society. In spite of several worldwide economic crises, the Conservative hegemony was a period of prosperity and growth for Colombia.[3] Capital accumulated from coffee export was used to establish new industries, especially food processing and textiles, for the domestic market. Not surprisingly, Antioquia became the main center of this new industrial growth. Industrialization became possible in part because Núñez and his successors abandoned their predecessors' strict commitment to free trade in order to provide protection for nascent industries. This was in no sense a movement toward autarchy, for Colombian economic policy continued to foster and depend on the cultivation and export of coffee. Protectionism, meanwhile, never became a partisan issue because the Liberals also moved away from their earlier support for free trade.

Industrialization also benefited from the disruption of trade during World War I. Colombia's stable and developmentally oriented government was well placed to promote the beginning of import-substitution industrialization during wartime and to prevent the destruction of the industries when trade patterns were reestablished.

What the government could not prevent was the emergence of new social tensions and contradictions resulting from industrialization, in particular the growth of urban working and middle classes that were less and less amenable to control by traditional clientelist means. Whether one looks at the new labor unions, at the foundation of socialist parties, or simply at the accelerating growth of the major cities, the traditional order in Colombia was under siege by a machine of its own making (see Guillén Martínez, 1979; Ocampo, 1980; Peeler, 1977; Havens and Flinn, 1970). In 1930, under the additional stress of the worldwide depression, the Conservative hegemony came apart, and Enrique Olaya Herrera became the first Liberal president since 1886.

The period from 1930 to 1974 may be seen as a prolonged

and complex crisis of the old ruling class as it sought to meet pressures for democratization of the political system without losing control of it (Leal Buitrago, 1974; Guillén Martínez, 1979). The crisis exacerbated the contradiction between two postulates of traditional party competition: Whereas control of the presidency was of fundamental importance to a party and justified any measure to gain competitive advantage over the opposition, control of the population was of fundamental importance to both parties and to the ruling class as a whole and should not be endangered by reckless political mobilization.

Olaya's presidency of course marked the beginning of a Liberal hegemony. There was some partisan violence as Conservatives were progressively expelled from positions of power, but nothing to suggest that the basic rules of the party system would change. In 1934, however, Alfonso López Pumarejo was elected president, and he used his Liberal majority in Congress to enact reforms that would radically change the shape of politics in Colombia. First, López sponsored the creation of the first elements of a welfare state to provide government help to the distressed urban and rural poor. More generally, López worked to expand the scope and power of the state to promote modernization. The law was changed to permit free operation of labor unions and to specify limitations on the right of private property. The suffrage was changed, essentially to enfranchise the entire male population, who for the first time would vote directly for president in 1938. It was certainly not lost on López and the Liberal leadership that these measures held the promise of attracting to the Liberal standard a heavy majority of the new voters, thus assuring their continued hegemony under new rules for which the Conservatives were ill-prepared.

The picture was further complicated by the rise of Jorge Eliécer Gaitán, a Liberal populist orator who went much further than the patrician López in condemning the injustices of Colombian society. He consequently attracted widespread support among the poorer urban sectors of Bogotá and elsewhere, people who now could vote. Though Gaitán had given up the leadership of an independent socialist party in the 1920s in order to return to the Liberal fold, and though his rhetoric was populist rather than socialist, he still constituted the most radical assault on the established order in Colombian history (Sharpless, 1978).

The Conservative response to these developments was ferocious. The reactionary Laureano Gómez became the dominant figure in the party. He demanded a return to the Hispanic values and social hierarchy of the colonial era, expressed sympathy with Franco, Mussolini, and Hitler, and lumped Liberals with Communists as subversive of true Colombian values and deserving of suppression. The church hierarchy strongly seconded this Conservative counteroffensive, and traditionally Conservative sectors of the peasantry were goaded by Gómez's rhetoric into hostility to the Liberals.

By the late 1930s Colombian society was becoming highly polarized around the two antagonists, Gaitán and Gómez. Millions who had never before been called upon to participate politically were now being aroused by the conflicting rhetoric of these two leaders. The Liberal party itself was becoming steadily more fragmented. The division in the party between López's reformers and more traditional Liberals was compounded by the rise of Gaitán to the left of López. The reformist thrust of López's first government was blunted by his own party, and he was replaced in 1938 by the more moderate Eduardo Santos. When López was again elected in 1942, he did not seriously push to extend the reforms of his first term. Gaitán, however, had not become reconciled, and he insisted on running for president in 1946, even after the official Liberal nomination went to Gabriel Turbay. Eschewing the Conservative nomination for himself, Gómez arranged the nomination of the less controversial Mariano Ospina Pérez, but took care to retain the reins of party control for himself. The result of the Liberal split and Gómez's political acumen was a victory for Ospina

Pérez, although Congress remained under Liberal control. Thus ended the Liberal hegemony.

The political polarization, however, increased in intensity. The government, in cooperation with the Conservative party, began eliminating Liberals from positions of power, using intimidation and force when necessary. Still in control of Congress, the Liberals could and did resist. This was the beginning of the decade of La Violencia, partisan violence, particularly in the countryside, that progressively escaped the control of the party elites.[4] After the 1946 election, Gaitán had gained complete control of the Liberal party, and with a majority in Congress the Liberals protested and resisted the official violence. After the Liberals retained their majority in the 1948 midterm elections, Gaitán seemed certain to win the 1950 presidential election. Then, in April 1948, Gaitán was assassinated in downtown Bogotá.

The crowd tore his assassin to pieces before anything could be learned of his motives or connections, but the presumption was widespread that the government and the Conservative party were behind it. In the next days massive riots virtually razed downtown Bogotá and shook other major cities as well. It was an abortive revolution. The government would certainly have fallen had it not been for the cooperation of the recently eclipsed moderate Liberal leadership, which now stood to regain control of the party. Characteristically, when the regime itself was endangered, the Liberal leadership rallied to support Ospina and assisted his government in restoring order in the cities.

But the bipartisan coalition could not last in the face of Gómez's determined effort to keep the Liberals from winning the next presidential election. Within a year the Liberals again withdrew from the government; they ended by boycotting the presidential election, convinced they would not be allowed to win. Gómez won easily, and during his presidency the violence continued. If it was still partly official, it increasingly assumed its own momentum, beyond the control of either party. The political order was being torn asunder.

Remarkably, the Colombian economy continued to grow throughout the period of La Violencia (Oquist, 1980, chap. 6). The cities, centers of industry and services, were not as affected by the turmoil as was the countryside. In affected rural areas, violence often centered on either possession of land or control of crops. This meant that those who had land had to stay on it or lose it and, being on the land, had to produce a crop and try to keep it in order to make a living. Thus, paradoxically, agricultural production, most notably coffee production, continued even in the areas of the worst violence. As individual producers struggled in a situation of excruciating insecurity, Colombia's coffee crops continued to get to market, even if much of the time the proceeds went to bandits who had seized them.

The repressiveness of the Gómez government gradually drove even the Ospina faction of his own party into the opposition. In 1953, the Liberal leaders and Ospina pressed the commander of the army, Gen. Gustavo Rojas Pinilla, to seize power from Gómez in order to break the cycle of partisan violence. Although the Rojas government did have substantial short-term success in reducing the violence, it never totally eliminated it, and by 1956 it was on the increase again. This time, in addition to traditional partisan violence, village vendettas, and armed robberies, the country had to contend with violence from emerging Marxist guerrilla groups, which had evolved from some armed bands. Also, Rojas showed his intention to remain in power and to organize his own mass base to displace the traditional parties. That prospect proved sufficient to induce even Gómez to moderate his truculence and agree to a historic compromise with the Liberals. In 1957, the two parties united on an agreement for the restoration of constitutional rule under a coalition government and Rojas was overthrown.

The constitutional reform that embodied the National Front was approved in a referendum in late 1957, and constitutional rule was restored the following year, after elections for president and legislative bodies (see chap. 3). The National Front sought to eliminate the main cause of partisan conflict by eliminating the possibility of exclusion from office. The presidency was to alternate between the parties for three terms (twelve years—later extended to four terms, or sixteen years). All other elective and appointive public offices were to be divided evenly between the two parties. To guard against one party ganging up on the other, a two-thirds majority was required for legislation in Congress (changed to a simple majority in the late 1960s). No other parties were to be permitted to hold public office. There was, however, no restriction on factional competition within the major parties. In short, the formal institutions of liberal democracy were being restored, but with competition strictly limited and with popular political participation largely stripped of its meaning and, in effect, discouraged. The National Front was a regime of political demobilization. It was a reassertion of control by the traditional elites.

Colombia has been and remains a strongly inegalitarian society, dominated by a small and highly self-conscious propertied elite. This elite, with diverse regional and economic bases, has traditionally been divided into two competing political parties (Liberal and Conservative), which have monopolized political power in Colombia since the 1850s. That the parties arose is not surprising: similar elitist Liberal and Conservative parties arose in many Latin American countries in the nineteenth century. That there were two parties again is not surprising: the winner-take-all imperatives of a president-centered regime promote that alignment. But that the Liberal and Conservative parties both survived into the late twentieth century, presided over the tumultuous democratization of an oligarchical republic, and still dominate the political system *is* remarkable.

Two overlapping processes have been at work here that together have done much to define the distinctive character of modern Colombian politics. The first process is essentially cyclical: the dominant party's hegemony begins to decay; weakened by factionalism, it gives way to an opposition-dominated coalition; finally, in due course, a new party hegemony emerges. The competition between the parties, however, virtually required the parties to seek advantage by mobilizing previously subordinate elements of the population, thus threatening the cycle. The parties had been outstandingly successful as capstones of the old clientelistic system of political control, in which the mass of the population were no more than pawns, but they could not maintain control as the increasingly urban populations were mobilized as citizens. The political crisis of the 1940s and the violence of the 1950s were the results. The National Front was a determined and successful effort to demobilize and control the citizenry without formally abandoning liberal democracy's commitment to universal suffrage and a liberal political system.

## Costa Rica: Moderate Democratization of a Civil Oligarchy

In colonial times, Costa Rica was one of the most isolated and poverty-stricken of the Spanish colonies, lacking in both mineral production and significant numbers of Indian laborers.[5] The area was distant from the administrative center in Guatemala, and most of the sparse settlement was away from the coasts in the temperate and fertile highlands. Without a reliable cash crop (though cacao was of some significance for a few decades of the eighteenth century), the population never grew very large and even the elite never got very rich. Contrary to some of the mythology about Costa Rica (see for example, Busey, 1962; Monge Alfaro, 1980), however, there was an elite, which dominated the administration and such commerce as there was. These people certainly wished to be richer, and shortly after Costa Rica's painless independence, they found a way (Stone, 1975, chap. 1; Vega Carballo, 1981a, pp. 1–19; Vega Carballo, 1981b, part 1).

The way was coffee. Costa Rica became one of the first

countries to begin producing coffee on a large scale for export to Europe. By 1840 the country was already committed heavily to coffee production, which quickly became the most important export. Production expanded until the 1880s, then leveled off before spurting anew in the 1920s and 1930s. Thus Costa Rica was an established coffee producer long before Colombia. This was due to a favorable conjunction of several factors. First, the climate and soil of the central highlands were extremely well suited to coffee cultivation. Second, key elements of the Costa Rican elite were ready to enrich themselves through export (even though they lacked both commodity and market). Third, enterprising Europeans found ways to ship and market the coffee profitably.[6]

It would not be an overstatement to say that coffee transformed Costa Rican society. It provided an impetus that lasted into the twentieth century for significant road and railroad construction, yet it established a one-crop, dependent economy at the mercy of the British and German markets and their often wildly fluctuating coffee prices. Coffee cultivation tended to concentrate land somewhat more than it had been in colonial times, but not to the point of eliminating small farms. The larger *cafetaleros* (coffee planters) operated *beneficios* (processing plants) on which the smaller growers depended. Also, the smaller growers and landless peasants needed the seasonal labor on the larger farms to supplement their incomes.

Obviously this sort of economic structure provided the larger landowners with ready-made political clienteles for elections or battles. Moreover, these clienteles would be relatively reliable, productive, and conservative because a large proportion were landowners, and the others might hope to become so by colonization. This system was able to extract from the rural population the labor necessary for the accumulation of capital, while legitimating itself by means of the regime of small property. The economic reality of concentration of land and capital provided the means for such economic development as took place in Costa Rica in the nineteenth century, but it rigidified the economy by creating vested interests to block changes that might hurt the country's position as a coffee exporter. At the same time, the ethic of egalitarianism and self-reliance helped to lay the basis for the democratization of the political system.

But if the basis was laid in the mid-nineteenth century, democratization did not become a serious issue until well into the twentieth. Constitutionally, all regimes until the Constitution of 1949 employed variants of the indirect election: presidents (and sometimes deputies) were elected by electoral colleges, which were in turn popularly elected. The right to vote was normally restricted by literacy and property requirements, and the right to hold public office was restricted by higher property requirements. Stone affirms that the literacy requirements alone would have excluded 90 percent of the population in the mid-nineteenth century.[7]

From the abstract point of view of political economy, the entire period before 1949 was one of dominance by an agrarian-commercial capitalist class. Viewed more closely, however, the political process was marked by a series of conflicts between identifiable groups of persons within that class. One dimension of that political conflict consisted simply in the struggle for control of the government for the sake of the economic benefits and glory it might bring.

Each cycle was initiated by a succession of truncated presidential terms, disputed elections, and unrest. Typically, a large coalition of disgruntled members of the elite emerged to remove an incumbent president or defeat his candidate at the polls. Eventually, one person—perhaps a presidential candidate, perhaps a notable private person—would be able to assemble enough support to impose a degree of stability. The scramble for political control having been settled, the political process next centered on a scramble for access to the clientele of the leader. As long as the clientele was sufficiently broad and powerful, it could control elections and maintain stability. Those who failed to get access, with its rewards of public office and opportunities for enrichment, however, eventually moved into the opposition. As the opposition grew and became more assertive, the hegemonic figure tended to rely on an ever-narrower group of friends and relatives; this of course further enlarged the opposition. Ultimately, the cycle came full circle, and the hegemonic figure was himself eliminated (see Table 2).

The hegemonies of Juan Mora Porras and Francisco Montealegre were times of the more or less direct control of the country by elements of the coffee-planting elite. That of Tomás Guardia, and the interregnum that followed his death, marked a watershed. Probably knowingly, Guardia began the process that would topple the *cafetaleros* from their position of economic primacy and link Costa Rica much more directly to the world of international investment (for example, he laid the groundwork for a banana-export enclave controlled by United Fruit Company). Probably unknowingly, he presided over a diversification of the ruling class which would have the effect of removing the *cafetaleros* from the direct exercise of governmental power.[8]

Guardia and his successors were reacting to decades of policy oriented almost exclusively to the promotion of coffee. As early as the 1820s one finds a commitment in governmental circles to providing incentives for the cultivation and export of coffee. But these governments did relatively little in areas that did not directly affect the success of coffee export. Most of the population was allowed to remain illiterate. Far from acting to promote economic diversification or industrialization, they actually encouraged industrial imports. Overall, the public policies of the *cafetalero* period display an active commitment to the principles of classical economic liberalism: they actively promoted coffee exports in accordance with the principle of "comparative advantage" and showed a general sympathy for free trade as that pertained to imports. Social policy during this period was also liberal, but not uniformly so: the church

**TABLE 2**
*Periods of Political Hegemony in Costa Rica*

| Hegemonic Figure | Approximate Dates | Transitional Periods |
|---|---|---|
| | | 1821–24 |
| Juan Mora Fernández | 1824–33 | |
| | | 1833–35 |
| Braulio Carrillo | 1835–42 | |
| | | 1842–49 |
| Juan Mora Porras | 1849–59 | |
| Francisco Montealegre | 1859–70 | |
| Tomás Guardia | 1870–82 | |
| | | 1882–90 |
| Rafael Yglesias | 1890–1902 | |
| | | 1902–10 |
| Ricardo Jiménez | 1910–36 | |
| | | 1936–40 |
| Rafael Angel Calderón | 1940–48 | |

was harassed, but not repressed; education was favored for the elite, but neglected for the masses. In the political realm, the *ambiente* was similarly liberal, but if people could speak and write more or less freely, electoral guarantees were purely symbolic, and everyone understood that.

The dominance of liberal ideas should not be taken to imply a party hegemony on the Colombian pattern, though. If one takes parties as institutionalized organizations dedicated to capturing and holding control of the government, then nothing of the sort existed in Costa Rica at least until the last decade of the nineteenth century, and perhaps not until the foundation of the Communist party in 1932 (Monge Alfaro, 1980, chaps. 8–13; Schifter, in Zelaya, 1979, vol. 1, chap. 2). This is true even though the great Liberal-Conservative cleavage of nineteenth-century Latin America was present in Costa Rica. Because those of liberal persuasion prevailed before there was need to form a party, and because church-state relations did not become an acute issue until the 1880s (and only briefly then), the Liberal-Conservative split never crystallized into parties. Further, it may be that in a small country with a tiny elite and an unmobilized population, the need did not emerge for an organizational instrument more sophisticated than personalist hegemonic networks.

The period from 1882 until the civil war of 1948 is known as the "Liberal Republic," to distinguish it from the naked class rule of the *cafetalero* hegemony of earlier years and from the liberal democracy that has existed since 1949. The changes from the earlier period were not radical; rather they represented the accentuation of tendencies already present: economic policies were liberal developmentalist; efforts to limit the influence of the church were intensified; education received increased emphasis; and greater value was placed on maintaining the appearance of republican respectability and constitutional order in political processes.

Yet the Liberal Republic remained an institutional arena within which a tiny educated minority, subdivided into personalistic factions and parties, competed and cooperated in the control of political power. The political process was just as elitist as it had been in the *cafetalera* era, but more civil, or urbane. Ricardo Jiménez was the dominant figure after 1910, but he did not monopolize power or control elections as thoroughly as his predecessors. There was more room for genuine competition between elite groups, and the period saw the emergence of the first institutionalized parties. The Republican party, founded in the 1890s, became Jiménez's organizational instrument; it was taken over by his successors when he lost the hegemony in 1936 (Salazar Mora, 1974). The Communist party, founded in 1932, was led by Manuel Mora until 1984, but it really is an ongoing organization rather than a personalist clique.

The Liberal Republic saw considerable democratization of

political participation with implementation of the direct election of the president in 1914. Moreover, the Republican party, the Communist party, the Reformist party of Jorge Volio (active in the 1920s), and other more personalist parties all developed increasing capabilities to organize and mobilize mass followings.[9] On the other hand, whatever level of popular participation existed at any given time had no discernible effect on the choice of government. The increasing levels of participation legitimated the system without requiring it to change. Nor did policy change much. The economy remained oriented to coffee and bananas, the government's role in the economy continued to be exceedingly limited, and the notion of its intervening to change the social structure was still heretical. Only in the area of education did the liberal governments take an active role, and this was the center of their traditional, if not very intense, conflict with the Catholic hierarchy.

From the time of World War I, Costa Rica underwent social and economic changes that worked to undermine the Liberal Republic. In the populous center of the country, population growth and land concentration combined to create a growing landless sector in the countryside, less and less able to find lands to colonize. This in turn led to the growth of urban areas, especially San José. In the coastal regions the establishment of large-scale banana plantations brought with it an essentially industrial organization of production which relied on Jamaican laborers having no ties to Costa Rican life and culture. The banana zones were thus a fertile ground for labor organization on a scale previously unknown in Costa Rica (Salazar, 1981, pp. 55–57; Backer, 1975, pp. 13–14). In the 1930s the Communists proved particularly effective in labor organization, in spite of repression by both employers and a succession of liberal governments. The governments of the 1930s seem to have found no other way of responding to the unions, and to the Communists, than repression, which was ineffective.

A third area of social change should also be noted. The

liberal educational policies, in place since the 1880s, had produced the first literate generations among the mass of Costa Ricans. Especially when combined with the changes discussed in the preceding paragraph, this resulted in a population less amenable to the traditional modes of elite control. Moreover, the electorate expanded as more and more voters were able to fulfill the literacy requirements. Against such changes, the aging leaders of the Liberal Republic and their younger protegés proved for the most part unable to adapt.

Yet there was little sign when Ricardo Jiménez reached the end of his third presidential term that the political system of the Liberal Republic was about to change. Jiménez arranged the election in 1936 of León Cortés Castro, his minister of development, a lawyer and *cafetalero*. Taking office, Cortés also took over control of the personalist machinery of the Republican party, displacing the aged Jiménez. Cortés's policies tended to unify the propertied classes behind him and to accentuate the resistance of the Communists and their working-class supporters. He created a stronger central bank and fostered strong trade links with Germany. The latter action was viewed favorably by *cafetalero* interests because Germany represented a major coffee market and because a strong German element had married into and was closely allied with the major coffee families. Thus, Cortés found himself able in turn to assure the election of his own chosen successor in 1940, although his nascent hegemony would prove ephemeral. Indeed, in the end only the Communists ran a candidate against Rafael Angel Calderón Guardia, and he took office with support from all other organized political sectors.[10]

In the decade following Calderón's election to the presidency the forces undermining the Liberal Republic finally destroyed it and complex and intense political struggles created the contemporary liberal democracy. An understanding of the swirling forces of the 1940s is thus essential to comprehending modern Costa Rica.

A physician with Belgian Catholic training which predisposed him to the emerging Christian Democratic political movement, Calderón had gained prominence as a philanthropist and had enjoyed a conventional political career as a member of Congress and minister, loyally supporting first Jiménez and then Cortés. Cortés no doubt expected him to be a docile agent in the presidency. Instead, he turned out to be a shrewd leader and political innovator who totally upset the parameters of Costa Rican politics. He intended to be the new hegemonic leader, and he quickly used the powers of office, patronage, and corruption to capture control of the Republican party, leaving Cortés with no choice but to found his own opposition party, the Partido Demócrata.

In this sense, Calderón was simply the latest of the hegemonic leaders of the Liberal Republic, getting and holding power by the same means as his predecessors. That may have been all he wanted, but he proved unusually creative in seeking to strengthen his government against the challenges of his opponents. Not since Rafael Yglesias (and perhaps not even then) had there been a government whose relations with the church were so cordial and mutually supportive. This reflected both his Christian Democratic convictions and his personal friendship with Archbishop Víctor Sanabria. Calderón's government rewarded the church for its support by reestablishing religious education in the public schools and by allowing private educational institutions to grant official titles and degrees.

A second, even more important, area of political innovation was Calderón's explicit attempt to mobilize a working-class following, and to do so by means of social legislation benefiting the workers. Under the liberal regime the state had done as little as possible for the workers and the poor and, far from seeking to mobilize them politically, had repressed their organizations. In contrast, Calderón sought to appeal to the poorer masses by providing them with benefits. He showed no inclination actually to transform the social structure (compare Schifter, in Zelaya, 1981), but through the provision of tangible benefits he was able to transform the political system by mobilizing and capturing a new clientele. The keystone of his approach was the Seguro Social (Social Security), approved after a long struggle in December 1941. This involved not only pensions but free medical care and other services.

By the end of 1941, Calderón had gained some working-class and church support, but he had lost most of the backing of more established sectors, which had made him president in the first place. *Cafetaleros* and other employers feared that the Seguro Social would deprive them of paternalistic leverage with their workers, and more generally feared the increase of state power. Serious liberals, radicals, and socialists were uncomfortable with Calderón's alliance with the church. The open, remarkably obtuse corruption of many highly placed individuals in the government, including their complete lack of subtlety in seeking to control elections, laid the government open to criticism, both sincere and insincere, from its opponents. And of course the Communists, who had been alone in opposing him in 1940, still opposed him.

The entry of the United States into the war both complicated Calderón's situation and provided him with a way out of his difficulties. Even before Pearl Harbor the war in Europe had closed the German market to Costa Rican coffee. Latin American coffee producers were saved from disaster only by the commitment of the United States to purchase surplus stocks. Calderón's decision to declare war on Germany, soon after the United States did so, however, angered pro-German elements among the coffee growers, adding yet another reason for their disenchantment with him.

On the other hand, the wartime alliance of the United States and the Soviet Union meant that both great powers now looked kindly on cooperation between Communist and non-Communist political forces in support of the war effort. When, in early 1942, elements of the conservative opposition approached the Communists about collaborating in a coup against Calderón, they opted instead to offer their support to Calderón, in return for commitments to enact additional programs benefiting the workers. Two major additional programs that resulted from the alliance were a constitutional amendment embodying recognition of certain social guarantees as rights of the citizen and the Labor Code, which for the first time recognized labor organization, providing unions with some protection even as it regulated and controlled labor relations.[11]

By the midterm elections of 1942, then, Calderón's regime had shaken out its early establishment supporters and had acquired the Communists, with their base in organized labor, to supplement the Partido Republicano, with its control of the government apparatus, and the church hierarchy. The most important element of the opposition was the Partido Demócrata, the personalist vehicle of Cortés, which tended to represent the interests of the more conservative bourgeois sectors, such as the *cafetaleros*. A more moderate conservatism was articulated by newspaper publisher Otilio Ulate, who founded another party, Unión Nacional. The third major opposition element, broadly social democratic in orientation, would crystallize as the Partido Social Demócrata in 1945.[12] The two main constituents of that emerging movement were the left wing of Cortés's Partido Demócrata (Acción Demócrata, whose most prominent leader was José Figueres) and the Center for the Study of National Problems, a group of socialist intellectuals who had developed a fairly detailed program of social and economic reform and political democratization.

About the only thing that all elements of the opposition could agree on was anti-Communism: the presence of the Communists in the governing coalition was a major issue for all of them. The two conservative groups were opposed on principle to Calderón's social reforms, while the two social democratic factions approved of them. Indeed, the Center for the Study of National Problems might have supported Calderón, except that they strenuously objected to the corruption of his administration. Cortés too was critical of that corruption, but given his record, his condemnation of corruption rings somewhat hollow; it was more a matter of tactics than principle. Of course, all elements of the opposition were out and wanted in, but that shared status did not help them much in forging a united front.

The opposition ultimately was able to unite behind the candidacy of Cortés for the presidential campaign of 1944, in which he was heavily defeated by Calderón's chosen candidate, Teodoro Picado. The opposition made strong charges of electoral fraud and continued through the next four years to question the legitimacy of Picado's tenure. Picado's term was marked by almost uninterrupted political conflict, and the ruling coalition did not attempt major new policy initiatives; rather, it just tried to hang on. The position of the government became even worse after the end of the war in 1945. With increasing tensions between the United States and the Soviet Union, the Communists were an embarrassment to Calderón and Picado, while opposition spokesmen could increase their credit in Washington by sounding the anti-Communist alarm. The Communists were embarrassed by the corruption of their partners, but for both sides of the coalition the alternative was worse: to allow Cortés to return to power and demolish the newly enacted social programs.

The 1946 midterm elections, which again drew charges of fraud from the opposition, showed a decline in support for the government, but it retained a solid majority in Congress. Cortés at this point made a play to regain hegemony by offering to throw his support to Picado if he would make a complete break with the Communists. Had he succeeded, he would have restored full bourgeois control of the government, and he would have denied José Figueres an excuse for an insurrection (for he may have feared Figueres and the Social Democrats as much as Calderón and the Communists). Cortés's sudden death, however, ended this possibility of a bourgeois coalition.

Meanwhile, two other lines of action were being pursued by elements of the opposition. Ulate's group and some others continued pressing for electoral guarantees and aiming to defeat the government at the polls. Figueres, though supporting the electoral strategy, was also actively preparing an insurrection.

José Figueres, from a Spanish immigrant family, was a prosperous farmer who first became politically active as an obscure backer of Cortés in the late 1930s (Ameringer, 1978; Castro Esquivel, 1955). He first came to public notice in 1942, when a fiery radio speech by him criticizing the government's incompetence and corruption led to his being sent into exile in Mexico by Calderón. More or less at the same time that he began to conspire actively against the Calderón regime, he also began to systematize his political thought (Figueres, 1955). If one begins with the premise that, like Calderón, his central objective was to get and keep power, the pattern makes a great deal of sense.

From 1942 on, Figueres never stopped conspiring toward and preparing for a revolt against Calderón's regime. Even as he pushed for the creation of the Social Democratic party and for an opposition coalition with Cortés and Ulate, supporting united-front electoral strategies in 1944, 1946, and 1948, he was simultaneously preparing for rebellion. The evidence is very strong that he intended to be ready to seize power whenever the opportunity presented itself. An essential element of that opportunity, the exhaustion of the electoral option, finally came about in 1948.

As the 1948 presidential elections approached, it became clear that Calderón, in true hegemonic fashion, planned to secure a second term for himself (Aguilar Bulgarelli, 1974, pp. 167ff.; Rojas Bolaños, 1980, pp. 134–47; Schifter, 1979, p. 82). The opposition pressed for extremely strict electoral guarantees, and in August 1947, under pressure from a sit-down strike led by thousands of shopkeepers, Picado yielded. The Electoral Tribunal, which was to supervise the process, was to be composed of persons having the confidence of Otilio Ulate, the opposition candidate. The police would be under government control, but it is still remarkable that the government in effect yielded control of the electoral process to the opposition.

In the election, Calderón received 44,438 votes, to 54,931 for Ulate. The governing coalition, however, won 29 deputies to 21 for the opposition. Calderón refused to recognize Ulate's victory, accused the opposition of fraud, and demanded that the Electoral Tribunal annul the elections. The tribunal at length declared Ulate provisionally elected, but one member abstained on the grounds that not all votes had been counted. Among the irregularities was a mysterious fire that destroyed a significant number of ballots. Thus, however insincere Calderón's allegations might seem in view of his own record, they did have some plausibility. In any case, Congress, controlled by Calderón, voted to annul the elections. Figueres had his excuse. With his armed force ready at his farm, he declared that the revolution had begun, with the declared goal of affirming Ulate's victory.

The war lasted six weeks and led to the government's surrender after negotiations had guaranteed the safety of the persons and property of the outgoing regime, the maintenance of the social gains secured under Calderón, and assurances to the Communists of their continued freedom to operate as a political party (a promise not kept). Figueres's Army of National Liberation entered San José on 24 April 1948.

A junta composed of Social Democrats was set up with the declared purpose of overseeing the transition from the Liberal Republic of the Constitution of 1871 to a second republic. Figueres was the dominant figure and president of the junta. On 1 May he signed a pact with Ulate agreeing that the latter would assume office within eighteen months, that in the meantime a constituent assembly would be elected to draft a new constitution, and that Ulate would be the first president under the new constitution. In the intervening time the junta would rule by decree.

Although Figueres's ostensible purpose was to guarantee recognition of Ulate's election, some have maintained that he really intended to impose an authoritarian regime (Schifter, 1979, chaps. 5–6; Rojas Bolaños, 1980, pp. 152–53; compare Ameringer, 1978). His behavior, though, is inconsistent with that assumption. Figueres and the junta clearly did intend to push through sweeping changes in economy and polity and to institutionalize those changes through a new constitution of Social Democratic character. They did not intend to be merely short-term caretakers until Ulate's conservative government could be inaugurated. It is important to realize, however, that although Figueres did reach an accommodation with Ulate and his conservative supporters, *he did not have to do so*. It was not a situation that required bargaining. With the bourgeoisie in disarray, with the army defeated, with the Communists and *calderonistas* discredited and in exile, with the U.S. government and North American corporations backing the junta because of their fear of Communism, and with a complete monopoly of force in the hands of the junta, Figueres could have done anything he wanted, including setting up a personal dictatorship. Instead, he made his agreement with Ulate, presided over honest Constituent Assembly elections in which his party was humiliated by Ulate's, watched the Constituent Assembly reject the Social Democrats' draft constitution and opt instead for a face-lift of the old one, and handed over power to Ulate, the old-line liberal, as agreed, and indeed ahead of time.

During the course of the struggle against Calderón, Figueres and his allies had become committed to substantive and procedural principles of social democracy which have guided their behavior substantially in subsequent years. Substantively, they wanted the state to assume a guiding role in the economy and to assume responsibility for minimum standards of popular welfare. Pursuing these substantive commitments, the junta continued the major social and labor legislation of the Calderón period; in addition, it nationalized banking and electric power and endowed the state with the authority and mechanisms for guidance of the economy. The junta's draft constitution, proposed to the Constituent Assembly, would have further reinforced the idea that the state should be empowered to act in defense of the common interest.

Procedurally, the commitment to social democracy entailed a demand for an honest and efficient administration and for a political regime of free, honest, and universal suffrage and the full range of democratic liberties (except, in Figueres's view, for those who subverted democratic values, namely the Communists and the *calderonistas*; he did not think they should be protected by democratic rights). These commitments to the procedural principles of social democracy may be seen first of all in efforts to purge the bureaucracy and punish bureaucratic malfeasance (the bureaucracy was conveniently *calderonista*). A more important manifestation of commitment to procedural principles may be seen in the honesty of the Constituent Assembly elections (we can be sure they were honest because the Social Democrats did so incredibly badly) and Figueres's respect for the results even when they meant the death of the proposed constitution. Finally, the commitment is visible in the fulfillment of the promise to turn over power to Ulate, even though this meant a suspension of progress on various reform fronts. In effect, when the substantive goals of the Social Democrats conflicted with their procedural principles, Figueres and the junta opted for the latter. In doing so, they established precedents of civility and accommodation between opponents which made the establishment of liberal democracy possible after 1949, even as their actions also deflected their own thrust toward substantive social democracy.

The new constitution, reflecting Ulate's dominance of the assembly, departed only marginally from that of 1871, but the changes did move Costa Rica decisively toward liberal democracy. In particular, women were enfranchised for the first time, leaving a literacy requirement as the only major restriction on franchise. Second, a fully independent Supreme Elections Tribunal was created to supervise the electoral process and isolate it from charges of partisan fraud. Immediate reelection was prohibited for members of the Legislative Assembly as well as for the president. On the darker side, the operations of the Communist party were constitutionally prohibited (a restriction not lifted until 1970). In effect the more radical pretensions of the Social Democrats were frustrated, but at the same time the liberals of Ulate became convinced that a liberal democracy was inevitable. With the promulgation of the Constitution and the inauguration of Ulate in 1949, the era of liberal democracy in Costa Rica began.

In summary, coffee transformed Costa Rica from a poverty-stricken backwater into a moderately prosperous export economy. As prosperity rippled out to transform the society, the political system soon ceased to be the exclusive preserve of the *cafetaleros*. The political leaders of the Liberal Republic were urbane, sophisticated modernizers. But stable parties transcending personal clienteles did not arise in Costa Rica during the Liberal Republic (Communists excepted), perhaps because political life was so uncomplicated that such parties were not necessary to getting and keeping political power. Politics in the Liberal Republic were built around personal, rather than party, hegemonies. In the course of the twentieth century, the Costa Rican elite evolved a political process that was usually genteel and non-violent, even when a hegemony was being challenged. Only independent political and economic demands from workers were regularly repressed. At the elite level, habits of civility were formed.

This elite civility broke down in civil war in 1948, after Rafael Angel Calderón Guardia sought to assure his political dominance by mobilizing a working-class following. As we have seen, resistance of propertied interests, widespread anti-Communism (reinforced by the United States after

World War II), and revulsion against the regime's corruption all combined to force Calderón out of power in 1948. But the regime founded in 1949 by the conservative and Social Democratic victors did not eliminate the social programs founded by Calderón. Other measures were added to strengthen the economic leverage of the state and to confirm its liberal democratic character. Civility was reestablished on this new ground between Figueres's Social Democrats and Ulate's Unión Nacional, providing the basis for a stable liberal democracy.

## Venezuela: Praetorianism, Petroleum, and Politicization[13]

At the end of the colonial period the Captaincy General of Venezuela was moderately prosperous, due to a thriving cacao trade centered in the valleys around Caracas. The rest of the country was not so fortunate. Caracas was the seat of a dynamic and self-confident creole elite with both agricultural and commercial interests, one which harbored steadily increasing resentments against the restrictions imposed by Spanish imperial authorities on the economic and political autonomy of the colony. Caracas—along with Buenos Aires —was the first colony to assert independence in reaction to the Napoleonic occupation of Spain. Leading this movement were members of the elite (notably Francisco de Miranda and Simón Bolívar) who had imbibed deeply the thought of the Enlightenment and the great revolutions of France and the United States.[14]

But independence did not come easily for Venezuela. The struggle was to a great degree a civil war; initially, in fact, it was a class war between the landowning and commercial elite of Caracas and the masses of poor plainsmen (*llaneros*), who so feared domination by the Caracas elite that they clung to the royalist cause. Only with the rise of José Antonio Páez from among the *llaneros* was there a leader able to bring them to the side of independence. The many battles fought in Venezuela and the commitment of Venezuelan armies under Bolívar to the independence struggle in places as far away as Upper Peru (now Bolivia) meant that society, economy, and polity were completely prostrated by the wars. Unlike the elite of Nueva Granada, which retained enough power to control the society after independence, the landed and commercial elite of Caracas was decimated and bankrupt.

If the Caracas elite was to retain any trace of its former preeminence, it was necessary simultaneously to find a way to maintain political control and to foster renewed economic activity. The political problem was dealt with for a century through *caudillismo*, which in the Venezuelan case meant a succession of ruling alliances between elements of the Caracas elite and a self-made military-political leader who managed to achieve dominance over other regional caudillos.

> Anyone could volunteer for the role of caudillo. It required ambition, the simple will to command, a sense of grievance, or the conviction that change had to be made in government. Caudillos depended on the three leading elements of society. Rural landowners provided supplies and much of the manpower, albeit not always willingly. Professional men manipulated the ideology, formed programs, and made plans. The commercial and financial sector of the towns and cities generated funds and the hardware of war. (Gilmore, 1965, p. 53.)

Beginning with Páez himself, who allied with elements of the Caracas elite to pull Venezuela out of Gran Colombia in 1830 and who then remained the hegemonic figure until the late 1840s, Venezuela's history through 1935 may be seen as a series of such hegemonies. The country as a whole was an ecology of local hegemonies with shifting lines of cleavage and alliance. The caudillo who managed by force of arms to gain preeminence over his competitors was in a position to control the national government, with its much greater opportunities for enrichment. On the other hand, the member of the Caracas elite who guessed correctly which caudillo to back, would be rewarded by access to government patronage, favoritism, and protection so long as that caudillo held power. Since resources were never sufficient to co-opt every member of the elite and regional caudillo, or to repress them all, revolts were common, indeed almost incessant, and some succeeded in replacing one hegemony with another.

Venezuelan *caudillismo* resembled both the Colombian party hegemonies and the Costa Rican personal hegemonies. The dominant figure—by no means always the president—was able to arrange elections in order to decide who would be president and what the basic policies of the regime would be. The Venezuelan hegemonies were eminently more personal than those of Colombia and distinctly more violent than those of Costa Rica, but the general idea of domination masked by liberal institutions is the same in all three cases.

The problem of renewing economic activity was solved, as it was in Costa Rica, by the development of the coffee industry (Carvallo and de Hernández, 1979b). Venezuela, too, was among the earliest countries to commit itself on a large scale to coffee cultivation and export; indeed, by the late nineteenth century, Venezuela was the world's leading exporter. Cultivation started around Caracas and gradually migrated southwestward up the Andes, specifically into the far southwestern state of Táchira (adjacent to the Santander area of Colombia, where serious coffee cultivation began in that country). Coffee was the mainstay of the export economy until the advent of petroleum in the 1920s. It supported the merchants of Caracas and Maracaibo, as well as large and small growers, processors, and merchants all along the mountains from Caracas to the Colombian border. Other than subsistence and local market agriculture, the only other significant economic activity was a very primitive sort of cattle herding on the plains of the Orinoco, primarily for export of hides.

None of these economic activities substantially reduced inequality in land tenure; if anything, they may have increased such inequality (as in Costa Rica). The economic impact of *caudillismo* may have been to make landowner-ship more fluid than in Colombia or Costa Rica by giving humbly-born men the opportunity to vault into the elite and acquire property as a consequence of their feats of arms. But even if ownership shifted, distribution of land and other property remained highly unequal.

Between the late 1840s and the mid-1860s, Venezuelan politics rather resembled those of Colombia, in that both countries saw the emergence of incipient political parties, Liberals and Conservatives, representing competing elite factions seeking control of the national government. The Venezuelan parties were, if this is possible, even less ideo-logical than those of Colombia. Rather, the partisans of Páez came to call themselves Conservatives, and their opponents adopted the Liberal label (and some of the rhetoric). The Liberals came into the government after 1848, when Páez's chosen instrument, José Tadeo Monagas, turned against him and embraced the opposition. But Monagas's autocratic be-havior finally touched off a revolt which ballooned into the Federal Wars of 1858–63. The definitive defeat of Páez in the wars also turned out to be the destruction of the Conserva-tives as an ongoing, organized force. And although every successive government of Venezuela thereafter proclaimed itself in some obscure sense to be Liberal, that party also ceased to have any real existence.[15] After 1863 the struggle for political power in Venezuela was personalistic, eco-nomic, and regional, but not partisan.

As with Costa Rica, it is possible to summarize Venezu-elan political history as a series of personal hegemonies and transitional periods, but with a larger, more diverse country, it is important to add the regional dimension. Of the list in Table 3, doubtless the two most important in their impact

TABLE 3
*Periods of Political Hegemony in Venezuela*

| Hegemonic Figure | Approximate Date | Regional Base | Transitional Periods |
|---|---|---|---|
| José Antonio Páez | 1830–48 | Llanos | |
| José Tadeo Monagas | 1848–58 | East | |
| | | | 1858–63 |
| Juan C. Falcón | 1863–68 | West | |
| | | | 1868–70 |
| Antonio Guzmán Blanco | 1870–88 | Caracas | |
| | | | 1888–92 |
| Joaquín Crespo | 1892–98 | Llanos | |
| | | | 1898–99 |
| Cipriano Castro | 1899–1908 | Andes | |
| Juan Vicente Gómez | 1908–35 | Andes | |

on modern Venezuela are Guzmán Blanco and Gómez. Guzmán combined a remarkable ability to get and keep power within the *caudillismo* of Venezuelan politics with an equal ability to operate in the cosmopolitan world of the North Atlantic (Wise, 1951; Juan Uslar Pietri, 1975; Lombardi, 1982; Gilmore, 1965). He saw that if Venezuela was to achieve prosperity as a supplier of coffee and other raw materials to the world economy, it would have to have internal peace, a strong state, and a much-improved infrastructure. His success in achieving the first was limited, but he had substantially accomplished his other two objectives. The state achieved a certain permanence of civil and military organization under Guzmán that it had lacked before, while port and transportation facilities were much improved. Caracas itself he transformed from an overgrown colonial town into a European-style city with grand parks, boulevards, public buildings, and monuments to himself. He never eliminated the power bases of the regional caudillos, however, so that he or his agents had frequently to deal with threats to his hegemony from aspiring rivals. Guzmán finally tired of living in two worlds and in 1888 retired to Europe for the last time.

As mentioned previously, Venezuela was the world's leading exporter of coffee in the late nineteenth century, with production centered in the Andean state of Táchira. The Andeans had played only minor roles in the chaotic politics of *caudillismo*, instead devoting most of their energies to production (including very early petroleum enterprise; see Velázquez, 1981) and commerce. But population growth and the leveling off of coffee production reduced the level of prosperity in the Andes in the 1890s, providing a pool of restless and discontented men to follow Cipriano Castro in a successful assault on national power in 1899. Castro's main lieutenant was Juan Vicente Gómez, who used the occasion of Castro's departure for Europe for medical treatment to seize power for himself.[16]

Whereas Guzmán Blanco had a vision of national transformation which he realized only imperfectly, the shrewd but unlettered Gómez had very little vision of the future of his country, but his dictatorship nevertheless saw fundamental changes. Gómez turned out to be the perfect, and therefore the ultimate, caudillo. His actions were systematically directed to what was necessary to keep himself secure in power and to gain for himself, his friends, and relations the material benefits of power. He insisted that his army be personally loyal to him, but he also insisted that it be professionally trained and led by career officers. Such a force was able, over the course of time, to destroy the independent power of every regional caudillo and to reduce him to the choice of exile or subordination to the national government of Gómez. The social basis of *caudillismo* was thus destroyed by this ultimate caudillo. Much as he would want his own private ranch properly administered, Gómez worked to strengthen the administrative capacity of the state and to enhance its fiscal resources. Again, all this was intended to serve the personal interests of the dictator, but he left behind a much more modern and capable state apparatus than he had taken over in 1908. He also facilitated the modernization of society, fostering growth of the infrastructure and the beginning of mass public education, up through the university level.

The wherewithal for many of these transformations came from petroleum, which the country began exploiting on a large scale after World War I. By modern standards, Gómez was exceedingly generous with the foreign corporations seeking concessions to exploit the massive fields under Lake Maracaibo; almost all of the profits in those first decades left the country. Yet even so, and beyond the private graft that attended the business, Gómez also secured for the state itself a volume of revenue far larger than anything Venezuela had seen before (compare McBeth, 1983).

Gómez did not really anticipate or understand most of these changes, and some of them were quite unwanted. The oil industry spawned a small but highly self-conscious proletariat. Oil money filtering through the economy fostered commerce and services of all sorts, greatly enlarging the urban middle class. The bourgeoisie itself expanded greatly with the new business opportunities. All this meant the beginning of rapid urban growth. Education inevitably brought new ideas and aspirations along with skills that were useful to the society. Professionalization produced younger officers who resented having to act as Gómez's personal errand boys. A totally new society was emerging (Fierro and Ferrigni, 1978; for a comparison with Colombia, see Peeler, 1977).

As long as Gómez lived, these changes stayed largely beneath the surface, though, in retrospect, signs of emerging ferment were visible, most notably in the agitation and subsequent repression of the "Generation of '28," reformist university students whose call for an end to the dictatorship led to their own imprisonment and exile and to the closure

TABLE 4
*Post-Gómez Regimes in Venezuela*

| Dates | Description |
| --- | --- |
| 1935–45 | Continued control by the military and civilian heirs of Gómez, with gradual and controlled liberalization. |
| 1945–48 | El Trienio, an abortive social democratic revolution led by Acción Democrática, brought to power in a military-civilian coup and overthrown by its former military allies. |
| 1948–58 | Military dictatorship of Marcos Pérez Jiménez and associates, with attempt to repress autonomous parties and other organizations; overthrown by civilian-military pressure. |
| 1958 | Establishment and stabilization of liberal democracy (see next chapter). |

of the Central University in Caracas (Betancourt, 1979; Martz, 1966; Alexander, 1982). Those forces for change would emerge even stronger after the old man's death in 1935, but if *caudillismo* died with Gómez, it would not be clear for some thirty or forty years what was being born (see Table 4).[17]

At the time of Gómez's death, it was uncertain who would succeed him or what sort of regime it would be. The minister of war at that time was Gen. Eliécer López Contreras, a veteran of Cipriano Castro's original march on Caracas and a loyal servant of Gómez. In close cooperation with other major figures close to Gómez, López Contreras successfully maneuvered the highly corrupt surviving family members out of the line of succession and arranged his own ascendance. Over the next five years a coalition of some of the more forward-looking of Gómez's inner circle pursued an effort to purge the state of most of the personalism and corruption of the Gómez period and to establish a functioning constitutional regime to replace the arbitrary authority of the dictator. Organization of political parties and labor unions was permitted, but under tightly controlled conditions that did not permit either mass organization or a direct challenge to the regime. In 1941, very much in the spirit of the highly elitist constitutional regime, López Contreras arranged the nomination and election of his own minister of war, Isaías Medina Angarita.

The two main organized political forces in opposition to this post-Gómez establishment were the Communist party, organized clandestinely in 1931, and Acción Democrática, an outgrowth of the Generation of '28, which went through several organizational stages, legal and clandestine, before assuming its final form as a legal party under Medina in 1941 (Magallanes, 1973; Blank, 1973; Betancourt, 1979; Martz, 1966). The two parties were acutely competitive in labor organization, while Acción Democrática (AD) was particularly a pioneer in the political mobilization of the mass public. The response of López Contreras to these twin challenges had been first toleration, then repression when it seemed that the opposition groups were growing too strong or demanding too much. Although some of López Contreras's supporters among conservative Catholic university students responded to the challenge by organizing a new student federation (forebear of the Comité de Organización Política Electoral Independiente, or COPEI, of which more will be said soon), the president himself did not sponsor an official party while he was in office (Herman, 1980; D. Levine, 1981).

Medina Angarita pursued a contrasting policy in dealing with the opposition parties. He legalized them, allowed them to run candidates for office, and tried to maintain communications with them. At the same time, he showed no inclination to surrender his basic control over the political system; indeed, Medina broke with López Contreras rather than permit him to continue as the hegemonic figure. Opposed on the left by the Communists and AD, beset on the right by López Contreras, Medina Angarita found himself in a situation quite similar to that of his contemporary Calderón Guardia in Costa Rica, and like Calderón, he found a way out in the international climate of World War II: he forged an alliance with the Communists under which they would support his government in return for privileged access to organized labor.

The social democratic leaders of AD (Rómulo Betancourt and others), already strongly anti-Communist, were outraged by what they saw as an opportunistic Communist effort to gain predominance in organized labor by means of a deal with the bourgeois, conservative government of Medina. At the same time, they continued to press Medina to accelerate the democratization of the political system by moving to universal suffrage and direct presidential elections. Characteristically, Medina kept talking, but in the end would not go so far as to sponsor an immediate change to direct voting for president in the next elections (1946). He and the AD leadership did agree on a joint presidential candidate who was committed to making that change during his term, but when the chosen candidate suddenly died, Medina backed a substitute not acceptable to AD.

Meanwhile, the AD leadership had been approached by a group of junior army officers discontented with the slow pace of professionalization, modernization, and individual advancement within the service. The officers proposed that AD join the military conspiracy in a coup d'état against Medina. Though this was of course contrary to the democratic principles of AD, after negotiations with Medina broke down, the AD leadership apparently decided there was no other way to break the hegemony of the post-Gómez oligarchy. A successful coup took place on 18 October 1945, inaugurating a three-year reform government known as the Trienio.

Rómulo Betancourt was made president of a revolutionary junta composed of five pro-AD civilians and two military men. The military leaders of the coup left the reform of civil society to AD, while AD avoided involvement in the administration of the armed forces. Although the latter restriction proved very important later, what was immediately relevant was that AD had a free hand to carry out its social democratic program of economic, social, and political reforms. Politically, the country was abruptly transformed by fiat from Medina's vaguely liberal oligarchy to a liberal democracy with free, competitive elections and universal suffrage. The first three such elections in Venezuelan history took place between 1946 and 1948. Those elections are generally thought to have been honest, but AD won overwhelmingly (though by declining margins) each time. The AD margin was probably due to its head start over other parties in organization.

Major social and economic initiatives of the Trienio included the country's first agrarian reform, laws facilitating labor organization, and a sharp upward revision in royalties paid by the oil companies, among many other changes. If the total package fell far short of a total revolution, the intent was to overcome the inflexibility of society and polity in order to transform Venezuela into a democracy.

Although AD had massive popular support (by default, because no one else was as well organized to seek it), the party had almost no support among the elite outside its own membership. The conservative and liberal wings of the post-Gómez establishment included the most important commercial and landed interests, and all were enraged by their forcible expulsion from the centers of power. Leaders of rival parties, from Communists on the left to COPEI on the right, feared that they were witnessing the establishment of a self-perpetuating AD hegemony that would permanently exclude them from power and office. The new leadership of the armed forces, meanwhile, having helped to put AD in power, came to mistrust AD's reformism and to fear the independent power of its mass base. Thus, slightly more than three years after overthrowing Medina, the same officers stepped in to replace the AD government with a military one. Virtually all organized sectors, outside of AD and its allies among organized labor and peasants, applauded.

After two or three years of jockeying for power within the military regime, Marcos Pérez Jiménez emerged with undisputed hegemony, confirmed when he heavy-handedly imposed his own victory in presidential elections in 1952. (Pérez Jiménez manipulated the vote count to deny victory to Jóvito Villalba, covertly supported by the outlawed AD.) The military regime, and in particular Pérez Jiménez's personal dictatorship (Kolb, 1974; Burggraaff, 1972; Rivas Rivas, 1961), was characterized by political repression. Elements driven to join the outlawed AD in the underground opposition included first the Communists, later Villalba's Unión Republicana Demócrata (URD), and finally COPEI. Further, by 1956 and 1957 important elements of the old post-Gómez establishment (initially among the strongest supporters of the military regime) had become disillusioned with its violence, corruption, and wastefulness.

If politically the regime was repressive, it did manage important economic advances.[18] A beginning was made on developing iron and steel industries adjacent to the huge ore deposits and hydroelectric power of the Lower Orinoco Basin, and a petrochemical industry was also begun. These major steps came on top of the beginnings of import substitution industrialization in the 1940s and basic food and textile production, which went back even further. The industrialization of Venezuela on a large scale, however, began in the 1950s. The regime also sponsored a massive construction program in Caracas, building high-rise public housing, new roads and highways, and other public works. Thus, in spite of its venality the military regime was a period of bonanza for many businesses, and many of the poor in Caracas remembered Pérez Jiménez as the president who built the "superbloques" of public housing.

Still, by 1957 most people, including most of the elite,

had had enough. Some lessons had been learned about the costs of sectarianism and the art of finding common ground. Cadres of the old enemies, AD and the Communist party, worked together in the underground resistance to Pérez Jiménez during the 1950s. Meanwhile, at the leadership level the major non-Communist parties—AD, COPEI, URD —worked out an agreement to hold free and competitive elections under a new constitutional regime and to form a tripartite coalition, regardless of who won the election. They agreed, in effect, that the establishment and mainte-nance of a liberal democratic regime was more important than the substantive programs of any one party. On the other hand, the exclusion of the Communists from the agreement was a sign of the boundaries that would be im-posed on policy under the new regime. The military high command, increasingly embarrassed by the excesses of Pé-rez Jiménez, was only too happy to support the parties' united front and to respond to a series of strikes and disor-ders directed against the regime by forcing Pérez Jiménez to resign and leave the country on 23 January 1958. A provi-sional government led by Adm. Wolfgang Larrazábal would oversee the transition to liberal democracy in the course of the next year, working closely with the party leaders (com-pare Sonntag, 1979; Carvallo and de Hernández, 1979a).

In summary, the coffee economy of Táchira gave Castro and Gómez the means to capture the national government in Caracas, but it was petroleum that gave Gómez the power to stay there by strengthening the state and undermining the foundations of potential opponents. The changes Gómez unknowingly set in motion were contained for a decade by his civil and military heirs. The dissident reformers of AD took over in 1945, intent on a rapid democratization of the country by fiat. But they lacked control over key centers of resistance in the armed forces, the economic sector, and ri-val political parties. The democratizing revolution of AD overreached itself, making way for a military regime in 1948.

The termination of the Pérez Jiménez regime and the establishment of a liberal democracy in 1958 were the result of a new spirit of accommodation between formerly hostile elites. There was an explicit understanding that, regardless of electoral outcomes, the vital interests of key political and economic sectors would not be threatened. This included not only the three main political parties (AD, COPEI, URD) but business, agriculture, and the armed forces themselves. The liberal democratic regime was founded on a mutual pledge not to rock the boat as AD had done between 1945 and 1948.

Even as the liberal democratic regime was being founded, however, the Venezuelan elites remained noticeably fragmented. The business elites still resented AD for its overthrow of the post-Gómez establishment in 1945, and more generally they scorned and distrusted the whole democratic system of competing, mass-based political parties. Rather than support any party, or found their own, the business elite tended to stand aside from the process, supporting a series of antiparty candidates (see next chapter). Thus, the groups that controlled the state (primarily AD and COPEI) initially had few firm links with those who controlled the economy. The armed forces remained a self-contained and autonomous elite which retained veto power over the political system without being committed to it, and the Left, dealt out of the original contract, had a choice of either submitting to permanent exclusion from power or rebelling. They chose the latter, becoming the first major challenge to the liberal democratic regime.

## Conclusions

Although the main impression emerging from the preceding analyses must be the diversity of the three cases, it is nonetheless possible to discern some similarities between them. Economically, all three countries had at least a minimal export capacity by 1900, exports which had powered a period of substantial economic growth in the late nineteenth century. Moreover, up until the advent of petroleum in Venezuela, coffee was the basis of the export economy in all three countries. We may say, then, that none of the three countries entered the twentieth century completely poverty-stricken and without the means to participate in the world economy. But neither were they among the most prosperous of Latin American countries at that time (for example, Argentina). Obviously coffee was of great significance in the political economy of all three countries, but it is not possible to attribute to coffee the *same* significance in all three cases.

All three countries have been characterized by great inequalities in land tenure, property, and income, but these are by no means extreme by Latin American standards. None has large numbers of culturally unintegrated Indians, but beyond that the three countries have strikingly different ethnic characteristics. In none of the three was there a particularly high literacy rate during the nineteenth century.

In matters directly political, behind the clear and considerable differences between the three countries in the nineteenth century, we saw what may be called a "patrimonial hegemony" as the basic mode of political domination in all three countries. Hegemony was personal in Venezuela and Costa Rica and partisan in Colombia, but the basic system was the same. Central to the legitimation of hegemony in all three cases were carefully controlled and manipulated constitutions and elections.

Anyone familiar with Latin America in the nineteenth century will see that none of these characteristics serves to distinguish our three cases from many other Latin American countries. In fact, there was little, if anything, about Colombia, Costa Rica, or Venezuela in the nineteenth century to set them apart from other countries in the region. What has set them apart, as stable liberal democracies, has to do with more recent developments.

The first step in moving away from the political system of patrimonial hegemony in all three countries was a period of masked hegemony, characterized by greater civility between rival elites, broader respect for civil liberties, less overt control of the electoral process, more scope for opposition, expansion of mass education, and gradual expansion of the suffrage. This phase corresponds in Costa Rica to the hegemony of Ricardo Jiménez, in Colombia to the last two decades of the Conservative Republic, and in Venezuela to the first ten years after Gómez's death. An important aspect of this phase in all three cases was the emergence of the first mass-based, persistent, relatively nonpersonalist political parties. In Colombia this occurred by upgrading the capabilities of the traditional parties. In Costa Rica the Communist party and the National Liberation party are rooted in this era (though the latter did not take final form until later). In Venezuela the Communists again, AD, COPEI, and the URD all began during this phase (slightly earlier in the Communist case).

Spawned by the greater liberality of the masked hegemonic regimes, these new mass movements were central to the violence that in each case attended the transition from masked hegemony to liberal democracy. The hegemonic regimes had become liberal enough to permit Gaitán, Figueres, and Betancourt to operate and organize, but none of them willingly became a liberal democracy. The details varied, as we have seen, but in the end it was the mass movements which installed the new regime in two out of the three cases.

Only in Colombia did the traditional parties finally prove adaptable enough to step back from the brink of oblivion, agreed on taking joint charge of a new, more democratic political system. Had the Liberal party remained united in favor of democratization in the 1940s, it might have brought it about while driving the Conservatives into a permanent minority position. Failing that, it took civil war and military dictatorship to convince the leaders of the two parties that it was both necessary and possible for them to coalesce to control a more democratic regime.

In Venezuela the deadlock between the democratizing reformers of AD and the heirs of Gómez proved impossible to resolve on the terms of either side. Both the Trienio and the Pérez Jiménez regime were terminated by military coups with broad support. In 1958 the rival elites finally realized that accommodations would have to be made. Only in Costa Rica might it be argued that accommodation was not really necessary between democratizing reformers and supporters of the old hegemony. Figueres's junta had an almost completely free hand in 1948. Yet accommodations were made in this case as well, with the circle of those included in the accommodations gradually expanding to lay the basis for a liberal democracy.

Significantly, in all three cases the armed forces were unavailable as opponents to the creation of a liberal democracy. In Costa Rica the army had been defeated and abolished. In Colombia and Venezuela the armed forces were at the critical moment anxious to liquidate military dictatorships and to facilitate a return to civilian regimes.

Accommodation, explicit and intentional, turns out to be the most important common element in the establishment of liberal democracy in these three countries. In every case the terms under which a formally democratic regime was set up explicitly protected rival economic and political interests. This was clearest in the National Front in Colombia, but explicit pacts of accommodation attended the establishment of liberal democracy in the other two cases as well. Rival parties were guaranteed access to power by means of a prearranged coalition in Venezuela. The signed agreement between Ulate and Figueres in Costa Rica guaranteed their parties such access, but only later were other parties admitted to the club. Conversations and negotiations between elites prior to the establishment of the regimes made clear that all would refrain from carrying policy initiatives so far as fundamentally to undermine the vital interests of any recognized elite. Liberal democracy became possible when the main economic and political elites became satisfied that it would not be used to do them harm. It may be that this virtually contractual character of the liberal democratic regime is what distinguishes these countries from those others in the region (for example, the Dominican Republic or Ecuador) that have had repeated, but usually brief, experiments with liberal democracy.

This emphasis on the agreement to constitute liberal democracy is congruent with the findings of such investigators as Almond et al. (1973), Linz and Stepan (1978), and Nordlinger (1981), who insist on the relative autonomy of actors in the political process in determining political outcomes. There is, in sum, little evidence that economic and social conditions have determined the emergence of liberal democracy in these cases, and considerable evidence pointing to the importance of particular political actions. The establishment of liberal democracies by means of explicit accommodations between rival interests is a similarity in process.

In conclusion, it must be emphasized once more that substantively the economic and political evolution of these countries was strikingly different. Many of the differences are obvious: the role of petroleum in Venezuela, persistence of the traditional parties in Colombia, abolition of the army in Costa Rica. Other differences are more subtle. Colombia began its industrialization decades earlier than did the other two countries. The weight and significance of coffee production varied substantially between the three countries, virtually creating modern Costa Rica, giving economic primacy to Antioquia in Colombia, helping the Andeans gain power in Venezuela.

Various combinations of social and economic conditions may *permit* the emergence of liberal democracy, but none determines it. These cases suggest that, at least in the culturally hostile environment of Latin America, the key factor is political: the ability of rival elites explicitly to accommodate one another's interests.

# 3

*The Maintenance of
Liberal Democracy in
Colombia, Costa Rica,
and Venezuela*

WE SAW in the preceding chapter that there are important similarities—as well as many differences—in the processes by which liberal democracies emerged in these countries. This chapter will analyze the manner of functioning of the liberal democratic regimes after their establishment, and will suggest that the regimes are fundamentally similar to one another, in spite of some important differences.[1]

## Political Participation and the Policy Process

From the establishment of the liberal democracies, the political arena has been formally open to virtually universal adult participation in voting and other modes of political action.[2] The only important restriction is the continuation of a literacy requirement for voting in Costa Rica, which excludes a disproportionate number of urban and rural poor. Given the 90 percent literacy rate of contemporary Costa Rica, however, the restriction is not numerically very important. Average voting turnout in presidential elections varies from more than 90 percent in Venezuela, to about 80 percent in Costa Rica, to 50 percent or less in Colombia. These differences reflect contrasting orientations of the systems toward voting participation. In Venezuela (since 1958) and Costa Rica (since 1959) voting is compulsory, and nonvoting citizens suffer difficulties in matters requiring official identification. Moreover, liberal residence requirements and the simple processes of voting in Venezuela and Costa Rica make voting relatively easy. The number of separate elections has also been minimized in these two countries: in Costa Rica, all elected officials take office simultaneously after general elections every four years, while in Venezuela the gap is five years (though in the latter country municipal elections were separated from general elections in 1978). Those who have made the laws and regulations want high voter turnout, which will enhance the demo-

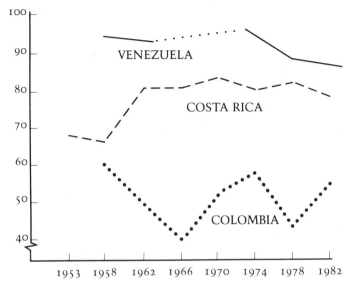

**FIGURE I**
*Turnout as a Percentage of Registered Voters*

cratic legitimacy of the system by involving most adult citizens in this symbolic act of consent (see Figure I).

The current leaders of Colombia can still remember a time when citizens were politically mobilized beyond elite control. The National Front was set up explicitly to demobilize the population by eliminating interparty competition. Demobilization was further served by separating presidential and legislative elections and by making voting voluntary and the procedure itself difficult and cumbersome. Months before the election prospective voters must assure that their national identification cards are in order. If they wish to vote anywhere other than the place where the card was issued, they must go through a separate procedure. On election day all roads are closed, so that persons who need to vote in their hometowns must take three days off in order to vote. Furthermore, the actual casting of the vote is an elaborate procedure. In short, the Colombian authorities prefer apathy to a mobilization they may not be able to control.

Other forms of political participation vary similarly. The Venezuelan parties make use of far larger numbers of activists, with more elaborate and institutionalized organization and much more ample financing, than do those of Costa Rica or Colombia. This is the case even though the Colombian parties have deep and durable roots in the party identification of the citizenry. That the Colombian parties are almost immutable social institutions does not necessarily mean that they are effectively organized as political forces. It is a commonplace of Costa Rican politics that only the Partido Liberación Nacional has even a semblance of continuing organization and capacity for mass mobilization, and by comparison with either of the dominant Venezuelan parties it is indeed a semblance.

Nevertheless, during the period of stable liberal democracy, all three systems have achieved a certain balance between the levels of mass participation and the capacities of the parties to organize and channel that participation. On one hand, the parties engage in competitive mobilization of voters and organization of activists for the purpose of winning elections. On the other hand, the party *systems* work to define, structure, and limit voter choice to a narrow range of options which are mutually acceptable to competing elites. In each case this party system has *evolved*, rather than simply being created.

In Colombia the two-party rivalry was limited and safeguarded by formal power-sharing and the legal exclusion of other parties under the National Front. With the resumption of party competition in 1974 many observers expected the traditional parties' dominance to end (but compare Peeler, 1976; and Ruhl, 1978). After the 1974 victory of Alfonso López Michelsen (Liberal), many observers thought that the Liberals would establish a durable hegemony, but a split in the Liberal party gave the victory in 1982 to the Conservatives' Belisario Betancur. Nontraditional parties receive only tiny portions of the vote, and only one of the traditional parties can win a national election.

A two-party competitive situation has in fact been the exception in Colombia: the rule has been one-party hegemony, with the opposition, more often than not, boycotting elections. The National Front was intended to put an end to that sort of violence-prone exclusivism. Since 1974 the governing parties have continued to allot some posts to the opposition, at the cabinet level and elsewhere. The question now is whether these measures to control and maintain two-party dominance of the party system will be able to avert either a reassertion of one-party hegemony or the emergence of powerful challenges from outside the traditional parties (see Table 5).

In Venezuela, Acción Democrática was still the strongest party in 1958, but Betancourt did not quite get a majority of the vote in the presidential election of that year. Rival parties and movements were much better organized than they had been during the Trienio. The elections from 1958 to 1983 witnessed three trends which together defined a party system increasingly dominated by two parties. First, the electoral support of AD declined through 1968, then rebounded in 1973, 1978, and 1983 to majority or near-majority magnitude. Second, the support of COPEI grew steadily to near-majority status in 1973 and 1978. And third, a succession of personalist, supposedly antiparty movements attempted with declining success to break into the emerging two-party-dominant system. These independent movements achieved their greatest successes in 1963 and 1968, while in 1973, 1978, and 1983 all such attempts to undercut the AD-COPEI dominance were ignominious failures. AD having converged on the center from the left, while COPEI converged on it from the right, their joint dominance of the electoral system confined the electorate's meaningful policy choice within a very narrow range, thus assuring a near-majority mandate for any president. Rival parties, particu-

TABLE 5
*Party Percentage of National Legislative Vote*

| Colombia | Liberal | Conservative | ANAPO | All Left | Total |
|---|---|---|---|---|---|
| 1974 | 55.6 | 32.0 | 9.0 | 3.1 | 99.7 |
| 1978 | | 39 | | 6 | 100 |
| 1982 | 56 | 40 | 1 | 3 | 99 |

| Costa Rica | PLN | PD | PUN | PR | UN | U | All Left | Other | Total |
|---|---|---|---|---|---|---|---|---|---|
| 1953 | 65 | 21 | 7 | | | | | 7 | 100 |
| 1958 | 42 | | 21 | 22 | | | | 15 | 100 |
| 1962 | 49 | | 13 | 33 | | 2 | | 3 | 100 |
| 1966 | 49 | | | | 43 | | | 8 | 100 |
| 1970 | 51 | | | | 36 | 5 | | 8 | 100 |
| 1974 | 41 | | | | 25 | 4 | | 30 | 100 |
| 1978 | 39 | | | | 43 | 8 | | 10 | 100 |
| 1982 | 55 | | | | 29 | 6 | | 10 | 100 |

| Venezuela | AD | COPEI | All Left | Other | Total |
|---|---|---|---|---|---|
| 1958 | 49.45 | 15.20 | 8.60 | 26.75 | 100 |
| 1963 | 32.71 | 20.82 | 0.86 | 45.61 | 100 |
| 1968 | 25.55 | 24.03 | 15.75 | 34.67 | 100 |
| 1973 | 44.44 | 30.24 | 12.44 | 12.88 | 100 |
| 1978 | 38.47 | 38.59 | 12.27 | 10.67 | 100 |
| 1983 | 49.97 | 28.63 | 12.10 | 9.30 | 100 |

Sources: Colombia: Registraduría Nacional del Estado Civil (1974), p. 182; ibid. (1978), p. 78; ibid. (1982), Boletin No. 24. Costa Rica: Tribunal Supremo de Elecciones (1969), pp. 18, 104, 189–90; 279–80; ibid. (1970), p. 43; ibid. (1974), p. 43; ibid. (1978), p. 170; Costa Rica, Gaceta (22 March 1982), pp. 18–19. Venezuela: Consejo Supremo Electoral (1969), pp. 24, 33, 42; ibid. (1974), p. 79a; ibid. (1978), p. 5; *El Universal*, 8 December 1983, p. A-1.

Note: Costa Rican parties are PLN—Partido Liberación Nacional; PD—Partido Demócrata; PUN—Partido Unión Nacional; PR—Partido Republicano; UN—Unificación Nacional; U—Unidad.

larly those of the Left, have been reduced to fighting for a share of the 10 percent of voters who reject the major parties (see Table 5).

Costa Rica has not developed the sort of two-party dominance that characterizes Colombia and Venezuela. Rather, what has emerged may be called a bipolar party system. When José Figueres turned over power to Otilio Ulate in 1949, he turned his attention to the organization of a party which would have the capabilities for mass mobilization so conspicuously lacking in the Partido Social Demócrata (PSD) of 1948. The result was the Partido Liberación Nacional (PLN), which Figueres rode to victory in 1953 and 1970, and which also won the presidency in 1962, 1974, and 1982. Two moderate political sectors have been consistently opposed to the PLN: (1) the liberal right, represented by Otilio Ulate (president 1949–53) and Mario Echandi (president 1958–62), and (2) the *calderonistas*, led by Calderón Guardia himself, who retain a substantial working-class base left over from the 1940s.

In the 1960s and 1970s those two groups moved toward burying their grudges and papering over their differences in order to forge a semipermanent, but perpetually fragile, coalition against the PLN. When this coalition was substantially united (in 1958, 1966, and 1978), it was able to win the presidency, but it could capture control of the Assembly as well only in the massive victory of the Carazo candidacy in 1978. Like AD in Venezuela, the PLN moved toward the center from the left, while the anti-PLN coalition first emerged as a rightist force (the *calderonistas* having largely given up their reformist thrust) and later moved toward the center with the candidacies of Carazo in 1978 and Rafael Angel Calderón Fournier (Calderón Guardia's son) in 1982. The parties of the Left, the Communists and other, younger parties, were banned until 1970; collectively, they still receive well under 10 percent of the vote. Thus in Costa Rica, too, the effective choices of the electorate have come to be quite narrowly circumscribed (see Table 5).

In its fashion, the Colombian system has been two party for more than a century. The Venezuelan party system, meanwhile, has become two-party dominant, even though it went through a period prior to 1973 when there was a remarkable proliferation of parties. Although since 1973 the legal left in Venezuela has had a significant role, that role has not involved serious competition for control of the government (see below for further discussion of this matter). Costa Rica, with its assortment of small opposition parties set against the large, centrist PLN, is of course not a two-party system. Nevertheless, as shown above, the Costa Rican system is certainly bipolar, with a broad coalition of parties normally allied against the PLN. If we consider two-party systems as a subset of bipolar systems, then all three countries are broadly bipolar (see Figure 2).

This is true even though all three countries use some variety of proportional representation for legislative elections. The tendency for parties to proliferate, commonly associated with proportional representation, does come into play: in all three countries large numbers of parties do get founded. This tendency is probably reinforced by the personalism of ambitious politicians who, after losing struggles to control their parties, prefer to leave and set up their own organizations, where they can be the bosses. The tendency to party proliferation has been checked in all three cases, however, by the overwhelming importance of the presidency and the "winner-take-all" character of elections for that office.

As a result of these conflicting pressures, the Colombian parties are faction ridden, but they do not fall apart, even though for most purposes the factions are the real political actors, not the parties. In Venezuela, more often than not, small parties append themselves to one of the major parties by endorsing its candidate, while running separate lists for legislative bodies. In Costa Rica the disparate anti-Liberación groups manage, because they must, to coalesce every four years, even though they lack the basis of unity to form

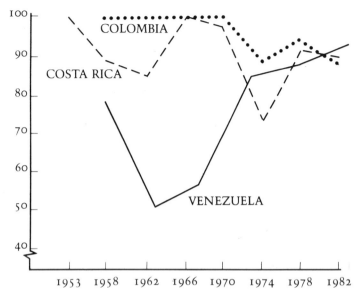

FIGURE 2

*Vote Percentage of Two Leading Candidates*

a real party. The durability of the current opposition federation, Social Christian Unity, is yet to be tested. And on every occasion when the PLN has suffered a major split, it has lost the presidency.

The bipolar character of these three party systems probably has a good deal to do with their stability. Bipolarity assures that any president will take office with an absolute majority of the vote, or very nearly so. The electoral systems of Venezuela and Costa Rica further strengthen the president by tying congressional elections to presidential elections and by having no midterm elections. There is, furthermore, the classic, self-reinforcing centrist tendency of bipolar systems. Confronted with the need to put together a majority, candidates and parties tend to avoid extremes because they fear rejection by the majority of voters. Knowing that only two parties have a realistic chance of winning and that those parties define the mainstream, voters simply do not take more "extreme" parties seriously. The parties create public opinion, and public opinion creates the parties; it is all very stable, as long as threatening new conditions do not arise.

All three countries display an active and diverse organizational life, which nevertheless does not penetrate effectively to the urban or rural majority.[3] Urban marginals, landless peasants, and *minifundistas* are for the most part not members even of the organizations that purport to represent them. As one might expect, this generalization is least applicable to Venezuela and most, to Colombia. Even in Venezuela, though, the majority of the population is not organizationally involved. Those who are involved in organizations are the economic and social elite, the professional and commercial middle class, and some regularly employed wage workers who belong to unions.

It is important to note that organized groups in these countries do not interact with the government in quite the way early pluralists used to describe pressure-group politics. It is not a matter of competing interests bringing conflicting pressures on governmental leaders, who shape policy in the process of reacting to the pressures. Latin American political systems in general—and certainly in these three cases— are much more centralized (Wiarda, 1980). It has often been pointed out that Iberian society is corporatist: that is, traditionally, it has been presumed that society comprises a diversity of interests which do have the right to organize themselves; the state has the obligation to decide which interests are legitimate and to coordinate those interests for the good of all. In a perfectly pluralist system, an interest group would want to be as independent of the government as possible (to maximize bargaining power); in a perfectly corporatist system, however, the goal of interest groups is to maximize its integration into the government (to maximize access to the pie that the government is cutting). Actual practice in our three countries is broadly corporatist, with varying overlays of pluralism.

The differences between the three countries in the way the very top of economy and polity are integrated are striking. Colombia is a rather clear-cut case of an integrated ruling class; very often the same people are leaders in various parts of the business world and in the parties and the government. The great leaders of the Colombian parties are, with few exceptions, drawn from families of longstanding and great economic power. These families have such diversified interests that they can no longer be identified as *cafeteros*, bankers, or industrialists. Given the persistent practice of representing all major political factions in the government (Betancur has done so), any major family can count on its interests being protected by the government (Hoskin et al., 1976).

Venezuela presents a quite different situation (Bonilla, 1970; Silva Michelena, 1971; Gil Yepes, 1981). First of all the country's main export product was in the hands of the great oil companies, whose relationship to Venezuelan decision-makers was one of negotiation, not integration. The Venezuelan economic elite, then, had to content itself with secondary sources of wealth, such as imports and exports. Under Gómez and his immediate successors, most of the economic elite had attached themselves to the regime and benefited from its patronage.

With the advent of the Trienio, though, those in control of the government had neither relationship to nor sympathy for the economic elite, and that sentiment was reciprocated. Even after 1958 one of the most striking and persistent characteristics of Venezuelan politics was the alienation and distrust between AD and the business community. Indeed, through the 1960s many important business leaders viewed the whole democratic system with disdain, refusing even to be serious about influencing the government, much less integrating themselves into it in the corporatistic manner. Only in the 1970s did accommodation take place between the government controlled by the mass parties (AD and COPEI) and the forces of Venezuelan big business. That accommodation came when business leaders accepted the fact that they would never again control the government, but that it was nevertheless legitimate and useful for the government to have overall command of the economy. The political elites of AD and COPEI in turn accepted the need to work closely with business in order to keep the capitalist economy healthy. If the relationship is less rocky now, the economy and polity of Venezuela are still in quite distinct hands.[4]

In Costa Rica the top economic elite of *cafetaleros*, merchants, and industrialists has traditionally been closely identified with one partisan current, the traditional liberals like Ulate and Echandi, while rather consistently opposing the PLN. From the latter party's beginnings in the 1940s, business leaders have distrusted its commitment to government command of the economy and its willingness to maintain and expand the welfare state started under Calderón Guardia. This basic division has persisted even though from the very beginning the PLN has tacitly ignored its more socialistic programmatic objectives in order to accommodate the interests of the economic elite. That has not attracted very many members of the economic elite to the support of the PLN, but it has kept conflict between that elite and the party at a minimum when the PLN has held the government (Arias Sánchez, 1978 and 1980; Stone, 1975; Carvajal Herrera, 1978).

Regardless of differences, by the 1970s in all three countries the top economic and political elites were working closely and cooperatively with each other in the formation and administration of economic policies that take for granted a strong guiding role for the state and frequently include state ownership of major enterprises. The basic thrust of these mixed economies, however, remains the creation of conditions for profitable operation of large private enterprises. The cooperative relationship is most natural and of longest standing in Colombia, where the two elites are one and the same. In the other two countries persistent tensions are submerged in the imperatives of cooperation to maintain the health of the capitalist economy.

These cooperative relationships have increasingly also mobilized international capital in support of the liberal democratic political systems. Industrialization for import substitution (most advanced in Venezuela; least, in Costa Rica) has led to the steady penetration of domestic markets by transnational corporations through nationally incorporated subsidiaries in each country. Manufacturing and marketing consumer and producer goods under license, these firms are often partially owned by local investors in each country, and their management has increasingly been turned over to citizens of the host country. Thus, at the top of the economy, where these transnational subsidiaries operate, the distinction between national and foreign capital has been blurred. The economic leaders who work closely with the government are as likely as not to be local executives or stockholders of a transnational corporation.

Within the frameworks formed by this cooperation at the top, the associational life of the three countries goes on. Each has formal umbrella organizations of businessmen, as well as associations for particular industries. For the most part, business organizations are independent of both government and parties and act as pressure groups to shape particular policies within the overall framework established by political-economic cooperation at the top. Typically, these business associations do not reach most small businessmen; hence, regardless of industry, the associations tend to represent the interests of national and international firms.

Associations for the mass population of workers and peasants show a quite different pattern. These organizations are normally at least loosely allied with a party. Frequently, rival associations are sponsored by competing parties. Thus, whereas the business associations act primarily to articulate the interests of their members, labor and peasant organizations work primarily to mobilize and control their memberships for partisan purposes. If the party that controls the leadership of an organization is in the opposition, the membership will be encouraged to engage in strikes and protests to bring pressure not only on employers but on the government itself. On the other hand, if its party controls the government, the leadership will normally work very hard to discourage disruptive actions, while using its access to the government to gain favorable policy decisions.

In Colombia the main labor and peasant federations are loosely allied with either the Liberals or the Conservatives. In Venezuela they gravitate toward either AD or COPEI, although the latter party is a relative newcomer to the field. In the 1940s and 1950s, AD competed with the Communists for primacy in labor organization, with the outcome basically determined by who controlled the government. When the Communists were allied with Medina, they controlled the labor movement. When Medina was overthrown by AD, the Communists were expelled from the labor movement and replaced by AD leadership. When AD was overthrown, the Communists were tacitly permitted to control the movement again for several years, before they too were forced underground. Under the liberal democratic regime after 1958, AD has dominated the movement (with recent competition from COPEI), while the Communists were at first outlawed and later simply marginalized.

In Costa Rica, in spite of persecution, the Communists have continued to dominate the main labor federation, based on their strong support among banana workers, which dates from their organizing efforts in the 1930s. The *calderonistas* also retain strong support among this group, dating from the 1940s. Surprisingly, the PLN has devoted relatively little effort to labor organization, except among government employees who owe their positions to the PLN's expansion of the state. Thus we have the anomaly of the *calderonistas* (fundamentally conservative, but with a working-class electoral base), more or less permanently allied with the business elite, against the moderately reformist PLN.

For the most part, the mass of the unorganized—unemployed and underemployed service workers and other marginal urbanites, landless peasants and *minifundistas*, and many small business operators—are simply nonparticipants

in politics, except, possibly, for voting. There are instances, however, of community organization among such
people, for joint action to improve local conditions, or for
demanding ameliorative action from the authorities. Sometimes these local organizations are strictly spontaneous; in
other instances religious or secular organizers may have facilitated their organization. Although this sort of thing does
not happen with enough frequency to challenge the political-economic status quo, that it occurs at all, against such
odds, suggests the potential for organization among the
least advantaged.[5]

The church is the scene of some of the most interesting
changes taking place in the 1970s and 1980s (D. Levine,
1981; Backer, 1975; Richard and Meléndez, eds., 1982). Of
our three countries, only in Colombia has the church his-
torically been strong (and of course traditionally allied with
the Conservatives). The church has been and remains sig-
nally weak in Venezuela, in spite of the presence of the So-
cial-Christian COPEI as one of the two dominant parties. In
Costa Rica, also, the church has been weak, but in the 1890s
and 1940s it played important political roles.

Regardless of its power, the church's traditional role has
been to defend the established order and traditional values,
either in alliance with a friendly government or as a voice
of opposition. Within the church's traditions, though, there
has always existed the basis for an alternative, prophetic
role of condemning the evils of this world, including social
injustice. Only rarely (as with Archbishop Sanabria of Costa
Rica in the 1940s) has the hierarchy been oriented in this
prophetic direction, but increasingly since the Latin American episcopal congress at Medellín in 1968, sectors of the
clergy and laity have relied on liberation theology and other
progressive Christian thought to guide reformist and even
revolutionary action. A major precursor of this tendency
was the Colombian priest Camilo Torres, who left the
priesthood to join a guerrilla band, and was killed in 1966.
More recently, in Costa Rica more than in the other two

countries, there has emerged a diversity of progressive religious groups engaged in activities from scholarly research to community organizing. This still is a minority current even within the Costa Rican church, but the high visibility of these people is a constant challenge to the more conservative hierarchy.

Especially in Costa Rica and Colombia, one also finds Protestant groups, of varying political complexions, engaged in proselytizing, health care, education, social work, and community development. They are not numerically impressive, but again are highly visible—and audible. The most prominent are frequently also the most politically reactionary, but there are those among the Protestants also who have been influenced by liberation theology.

## The Theory and Practice of Constitutional Government

We have devoted considerable attention to political participation and the processes of politics, but it is obviously also important to look at the formal and informal structures within which participation and decision making go on. Under the liberal democratic regimes, all three countries have explicit and extensive guarantees of citizen rights and freedoms, which compare favorably with those of any constitutional democratic regime. Yet in all three freedom of radical opposition (especially from the left) has been severely restricted and often repressed, largely within the law. Colombia has spent most of the time since the establishment of the National Front under martial law. This gives the president and the armed forces extraordinary powers of search and seizure, of arrest without charges, of military trial and punishment. These special powers have been used to combat persistent leftist insurgencies, but to date have not succeeded in eliminating them. It has been commonly charged in Colombia that the military has so much autonomy that it is in de facto control of the government. That may be an overstatement, but it is true that the High Command has until recently resisted all attempts to end the insurgencies by granting amnesties. Thus most of the Colombian Left only now has the option of the amnesty enacted under President Betancur and the opportunity for operation within the law (cease-fires are, in mid-1984, in effect or under negotiation with most insurgent groups).

Venezuela confronted a similar situation in the 1960s, when leftist insurgents actively sought the overthrow of the liberal democratic regime. The insurgency began in response to the conservative social and economic policies that attended the foundation of the democratic regime. Further, both the Communists and the left wing of AD were pointedly excluded from the exercise of political authority after 1958. These were the groups that took up arms (the latter becoming MIR, the Movement of the Revolutionary Left). The Betancourt and Leoni administrations (1959–64 and 1964–69) had for the most part defeated the insurgents by 1966 or 1967. Rafael Caldera, the first COPEI president, extended an amnesty which was accepted by almost all the fighters. By 1973, MIR, the Communist party, and the Movimiento al Socialismo (MAS, an anti-Moscow faction of the Communists) had all achieved legal status and contested the elections. In the course of the elections of 1973 and 1978, the Left achieved a durable status as the only organized alternative to the AD/COPEI hegemony. MAS is now clearly the strongest force on the left, but has not succeeded in absorbing or eclipsing the other parties. The Left is not, for the moment, a serious threat to capture the presidency, but it does obtain representation in Congress, and thus some public visibility. Having lost the armed struggle, the Venezuelan Left has accepted a minority, but still legitimate, role within the Venezuelan liberal democracy.

The situation in Costa Rica is similar to that of Venezuela, except that Costa Rica has not endured a full-scale leftist insurgency. Both Ulate's Unión Nacional and Figueres's

Social Democrats agreed in 1948 that the new constitution should prohibit the Communist party and any other party of similar ideology. That prohibition held until its repeal in the late 1960s; the Left first competed openly in a presidential election in 1970. The Communist party and other leftist parties were permitted to operate more or less openly throughout the period of the prohibition, but they could not run for office. It is impressive that the Communists were able to retain their base in organized labor during their period of semilegality. The period since legalization has seen considerable fragmentation on the left, and collectively these parties obtain an even smaller portion of the vote than their counterparts in Venezuela, but like the latter, they are the only organized alternatives to the centrist parties (see Table 5, above).

In a formal sense freedom of the press exists to an impressive degree in all three countries. In each case, however, the system does seriously disadvantage minority political forces. In the broadcast media some radio stations are partisan; moreover, because it costs money to advertise on radio or television, the established parties, with their greater resources, have the advantage. The printed press in Colombia is largely partisan. Both traditional parties have a number of papers around the country. The minor parties, even if they publish their own papers, reach only minuscule audiences. The Venezuelan press is mostly nonpartisan, but the dominant papers are *El Nacional* and *El Universal* of Caracas, both of which tend to be center-right. In addition to being unsympathetic to the Left, they are predictably biased in favor of AD and COPEI as newsmakers. The Costa Rican daily press also tends to be right of center (*La Nación*, the most important paper, is quite far right of center) and not very sympathetic even to the PLN. The Costa Rican Left, consequently, can count on no help from the press, except for its own low-circulation weeklies.

Turning now to the constitutional character of government itself, three characteristics of these three countries stand out. First of all, as compared with other Latin American countries, the president's powers are limited, not only in theory but in practice (DiBacco, 1977). While certainly not equal to the president's power, the legislative branch in each of the three countries does have and use the capability to force the president to bargain, and can on occasion defeat him outright. Even in quasi-democracies like Mexico or Brazil (since its partial liberalization) one does not lightly cross the president. The presidents of Colombia, Costa Rica, and Venezuela are strong figures, but not omnipotent. At least two factors may help to explain the ability of these countries effectively to limit the powers of the president. In each case the regime was founded in reaction to abuses of authority, and so there was a consensus at the outset on the need to limit the authority of the president. Once the regime was organized, the legislature invariably had strong representation from a well-organized opposition party, which retained enough common ground with the president's party to render its opposition partial, rather than total. In bargaining with such an opposition, the president did not need to feel that he was selling his soul. Indeed, between the leaders of the main centrist parties that dominate each system, there continues to be an ethos of limited competition within an overarching consensus.

It is inconceivable that liberal democracy could have been maintained in these three countries without two other formal characteristics which are most untypical of Latin America: honest elections and the regular practice of alternation of parties in the presidency. The establishment of liberal democracies in Costa Rica and Venezuela included the creation of powerful, independent agencies to administer the electoral process, agencies carefully structured to assure that neither the government nor any party could covertly control an election. These institutions have put an end to party or personal hegemony imposed through fixed elections.

Colombia, since the establishment of the National Front,

has done essentially the same thing with a less elaborate structure. The same organization that is responsible for providing citizens with national identity cards and keeping track of them also administers the electoral process, and the Registraduría Nacional del Estado Civil has been carefully insulated from partisan politics and patronage. In the National Front period only the 1970 presidential election was marred by charges of fraud, when it was alleged that the election was stolen from Gen. Rojas Pinilla, candidate of the Alianza Nacional Popular (ANAPO) and an opponent of the National Front. This was never proved, but such charges are by nature difficult to prove. In any case, if we compare the liberal democratic regimes in all three countries with periods as recent as the 1940s, the almost total absence of electoral fraud as a political issue is striking. As long as fraud is a serious possibility, trust between competing parties is impossible: to allow your opponents to occupy the government is to know that they will win every subsequent election until they are ousted. In the Colombian case, 1970 notwithstanding, the trust between the traditional parties has not been broken since 1958, though it was strained in 1978 when Betancur held back several days before conceding.

Though each country faced intractable social and economic problems, once electoral honesty, and the interparty trust that goes with it, had been established, it became natural for the "out" party in these bipolar systems to win presidential elections. The National Front, of course, mandated this exchange of power, but contrary to many people's expectations, the Colombian Conservatives did win the presidency in 1982, after eight years of freely elected Liberal governments. In Costa Rica alternation between Liberación and its opponents has occurred consistently, except for back-to-back PLN victories in 1970 and 1974. In Venezuela, after two AD governments, 1959–69, alternation has prevailed in the three subsequent administrations. What is important here is not strict alternation in each election but simply the probability that the "out" party will win an election and control the government in the near future. That knowledge goes a long way toward discouraging opposition conspiracies. And of course it provides an escape valve for the electorate: when things go badly for a government, as they almost always do, there stands the opposition, florid with passionate criticisms and solemn pledges to set things right (see Table 6).

## The Armed Forces

In a sense this book is a study of countries in which the armed forces are not running the government. We saw in the last chapter that an essential condition for the establishment of liberal democracy was the immobilization of the military. In Costa Rica this was done permanently by abolishing the army. In Venezuela and Colombia it occurred because the armed forces were anxious to avoid identification with unpopular dictators. This sort of circumstance occurs in at least one Latin American country almost every year, and the almost invariable result is the establishment of a liberal democratic regime. The harder question is, How has it happened that these three liberal democracies have maintained themselves for so long, avoiding a military takeover, when democratic regimes in most Latin American countries fail to last out a single presidential term?

The Costa Ricans are very proud of having solved their problem by abolishing their army, but that is a simplistic and rhetorical answer. They have two forces with enough manpower and weapons to take over the government should they wish to do so: the Civil Guard, under the Ministry of Public Security, and the Rural Guard, under the Ministry of Interior. Neither force has shown political ambition because, top to bottom, each is staffed by patronage appointees of the party in power. Indeed, the two guards constitute the main pool of patronage available to a government, since Costa Rica has a fairly advanced civil service statute cover-

**TABLE 6**
*Parties Controlling the Presidency*

|  | *President* | *Party* |
|---|---|---|
| *Colombia* | | |
| 1958 | Lleras Camargo | Liberal (National Front) |
| 1962 | Valencia | Conservative (National Front) |
| 1966 | Lleras Restrepo | Liberal (National Front) |
| 1970 | Pastrana | Conservative (National Front) |
| 1974 | López Michelsen | Liberal |
| 1978 | Turbay | Liberal |
| 1982 | Betancur | Conservative |
| *Costa Rica* | | |
| 1953 | Figueres | Liberación Nacional |
| 1958 | Echandi | Unión Nacional |
| 1962 | Orlich | Liberación Nacional |
| 1966 | Trejos | Unificación Nacional |
| 1970 | Figueres | Liberación Nacional |
| 1974 | Oduber | Liberación Nacional |
| 1978 | Carazo | Unidad |
| 1982 | Monge | Liberación Nacional |
| *Venezuela* | | |
| 1958 | Betancourt | Acción Democrática |
| 1963 | Leoni | Acción Democrática |
| 1968 | Caldera | COPEI |
| 1973 | Pérez | Acción Democrática |
| 1978 | Herrera | COPEI |
| 1983 | Lusinchi | Acción Democrática |

ing other government employees. The fact that the two guards are under separate commands presumably serves as a check on them, but it has also led to inconsistency and friction in dealing with the anti-Sandinista insurgents operating out of northern Costa Rica, as the two forces have come to reflect the conflicting policy stances of their respective ministers (*Mesoamerica* [1984], p. 9). Still, the threat of military intervention in politics is low because the guards are lightly armed, poorly trained, and politically appointed. The Costa Rican solution, in short, is to avoid professionalizing their armed forces.

Venezuela and Colombia obviously do have large and highly professional armed forces which have seized power from civilian governments before, but they have not done so since the establishment of liberal democracy. In both countries there have been attempted coups, but in each case the bulk of the armed forces not only refused to join but assisted in putting it down. The armed forces in each country have been well treated by successive democratic governments: military pay and equipment have been kept up reasonably well, and presidents generally avoid intervening in such internal matters as promotions and retirements. But that is not sufficient to explain the military restraint. The basic explanation, for Costa Rica as well as the other two countries, is that successive democratic regimes have thus far avoided either a political breakdown or an economic disaster which would provide *golpistas* within the military with the excuse, or opportunity, for intervention (Finer, 1975). The liberal democratic regimes thus far have achieved enough stability, enough legitimacy in the eyes of the population, that a simple seizure of power by an ambitious general in the absence of an obvious major crisis is no longer possible (Burggraaff, 1972; Maullin, 1973; Ruhl, 1980; Taylor, 1968).

## Economy and Society

All three of these countries are liberal democracies according to the stated criteria (compare Taylor, 1971). If participation is markedly unequal, if economic elites wield disproportionate influence, if the systems are dominated by
centrist parties with few real differences between them, and
if political rights and freedoms mainly benefit the mainstream, still we should remember that every one of these
criticisms has been directed with equal vigor at the United
States. It is not necessary to be fully democratic in order to
be a liberal democracy.

Virtually every one of the economic and social transformations that these three countries have passed through in
the last forty years has served to maintain or increase the
gap between haves and have-nots.[6] This can only be a major
challenge to their pretensions of democracy.

As modernization has proceeded in these countries, it has
taken place almost exclusively in the sector tied into the
world economy, while either passing over or bleeding those
sectors that are not assets for participation in the world
economy (compare Therborn, 1979). Those who have much
—great coffee growers and exporters, banana companies, the
state itself—are in a position to get more, while those who
have not—smallholding peasants, rural and urban laborers,
underemployed or unemployed dwellers in urban marginal
settlements—are at best passed over, at worst despoiled.
Subsistence, staple-producing agriculture is not nearly as
profitable as export-crop production; so the small farmers
tend to be driven off the land, either by denial of credit or
by more direct and ruthless means. Agricultural mechaniza-
tion and the conversion of farmland into pasture for beef
cattle eliminate jobs for rural workers. These people can do
nothing but to seek another life in the cities. Thus began
the wave of accelerated urbanization in all three countries
(Peeler, 1977; Bogan, in Zelaya, 1979, vol. 2).

These people were pushed into the cities because there

was no longer a place for them in the *campo*, the country-side. But the cities were ill-equipped to absorb them. Unlike eighteenth-century England, there were few factory jobs. So they just went, found or created housing where they could, eked out a living however they could. High birth rates and declining death rates led to rapid population growth, and because of migration most of the growth was in the urban areas.

If the great cities were no paradise for the marginal populations, though, for those higher on the social and economic scale they held great opportunities. The wealth from exports channeled into the cities and supported thriving commercial and banking activities, as well as the initiation of import-substitution industrialization. The latter activity was usually initiated by local capital (directly or indirectly a product of the export economy), with government support (for example, high tariffs and subsidies). Frequently, such industrial firms have then been wholly or partially sold out to transnational companies, presumably at a good profit. Further down the social ladder, middle-class persons also had opportunities for well-paid, high-status jobs in commerce, industry, and government. In short, modernization meant a distinct improvement in the life chances of the upper and middle strata, but not the lower strata.

Fueled by petroleum, the modernization and urbanization of Venezuela has been particularly feverish, and the gap between rich and poor, wide and visible. In Costa Rica, however, the crisis has been relatively mild for several reasons. In this small country, even rapid urbanization has not produced unmanageably large cities. There was less pressure on people to leave the countryside because there was actually a labor shortage well into this century, and even today the level of rural overpopulation is relatively minor. One does not find quite the depth of squalor among the poor of San José, as compared with Caracas. Still, San José and its environs have reached half a million inhabitants, most of whom are poor. It is a difference of degree, not kind.

With its long heritage of violence and its highly stratified society, one of the distinctive manifestations of persistent inequality in Colombia has been the high crime rate. Many areas, both urban and rural, have experienced high levels of violence against both persons and property, ranging from all aspects of the organized drug traffic to petty armed robbery. By no means are all of the criminals poor, but it is inconceivable that the Colombian crime rate would be so high if the majority of the population were not living near the margin of subsistence (Oquist, 1980).

These rapidly changing, markedly inegalitarian societies have endured the prolonged world economic crisis that began in the early 1970s, and is continuing. The breakdown of the world monetary system, followed by the massive petroleum price increases of 1973, put tremendous strains on the economies of Colombia and Costa Rica. Inflation and a balance-of-payments crisis reverberated through the two economies, lowering standards of living and increasing unemployment. Intensifying the strains, another round of petroleum price increases in the late 1970s coincided with a time of low prices for coffee and other major exports of Costa Rica and Colombia. Colombia's more diverse and self-sufficient economy suffered less than that of Costa Rica, which entered a prolonged crisis marked by accelerating inflation, an acute governmental fiscal crisis, an inability to meet foreign debts as foreign exchange was exhausted, and, of course, rising unemployment.

Interestingly, Venezuela, one of the main beneficiaries of the oil price increases, also emerged from the 1970s with a battered economy. The two waves of price increases pumped large amounts of money through the state and into the Venezuelan economy. In spite of fairly sophisticated efforts to manage these new resources and use them constructively, there were naturally inflationary pressures (virtually unknown in a country with the strongest currency in the Western Hemisphere). But the real problem came at the end of the 1970s and the beginning of the 1980s. The worldwide response to the OPEC price increases had reduced consumption and produced a glut; prices first leveled off, then began to fall. Apparently few people in OPEC (other than some Saudis) ever thought that would happen. Although Venezuela's difficulties were not nearly as serious as Mexico's in 1982, the Venezuelan economy did move into a recession, with falling output, rising unemployment, and government deficits.

In all three countries, the brunt of the economic crisis of the 1970s was borne disproportionately by the poor, who saw more unemployment and underemployment, rising prices, stagnant wages, and the loss of government services as a result of austerity measures. Those with more resources of course also suffered, but they were better able to protect themselves.

In a nutshell, neither development nor depression has reduced the deep inequalities or substantially lightened the burden of poverty carried by the majority of the population. The same generalizations can be made about other Latin American countries that are not liberal democracies. The presence of stable liberal democracy has done nothing to reduce inequality or eliminate poverty, while the persistence of inequality and poverty have not prevented the establishment of stable liberal democracies.

## The Liberal Democratic Polity

The reader will probably agree that inequality and poverty on the scale found in these three countries amounts to economic domination of the poor. Liberal democracy has not mitigated these conditions; in fact it has been an important factor in masking and legitimating that domination.

The establishment of these regimes was made possible by a conscious and explicit decision between rival elites to accommodate one another, rather than each seek a definitive victory. This pattern of elite accommodation has continued and even strengthened in the intervening years, becoming the foundation without which a liberal democracy could not have been maintained. In this sense, these three regimes have much in common with the European consociational democracies (though only Colombia has actually made use of a consociational mechanism; see Dix, 1980). In a consociational regime, rival elites, having mobilized potentially hostile publics for political competition, conclude that to avoid civil war some accommodation between them will be necessary. This takes two forms: power sharing between rival elites, as in a grand coalition, and policy restraint, the avoidance of measures that will threaten the central interests of any party to the accommodation. Each elite must maintain its political base by partisan appeals to its constituents, whose votes, in a democracy, constitute a mandate to deal harshly with the "enemy." Instead of acting on this mandate evoked by particularistic appeals, however, the rivals join hands so that none of them will seek to throttle the others. Thus is "democracy" preserved in a divided society.

Save for the National Front period in Colombia, accommodation in these Latin American democracies has not taken the form of prearranged power sharing; thus, with that single exception, they are not consociational regimes, though they are regimes of accommodation. Political conflict has not been eliminated, but rather contained or domesticated. Electoral outcomes are not predetermined, but are effectively confined within a range acceptable to the cooperating elites. Policy changes only marginally from government to government, oscillating around a broad consensus reflecting a balance of the dominant interests. This policy consensus in all three cases assumes that there will be a capitalist economy, based on export and promoting industrialization, with strong leadership and participation by the state. Further, the succession of democratic governments in each country has enacted only ameliorative, rather than structurally radical, social programs. Expansion of public education has been widespread, with the attendant growth in the literacy rate. Social welfare subsidies such as health care have made substantial progress under the democratic regimes (least in Colombia). The rural and urban poor increasingly benefit from public utilities (power, water, sewer). All three countries have had agrarian reforms, but enforcement has been spotty, with more emphasis on colonization than redistribution. Even Venezuela's well-financed program has not radically transformed land tenure. None of the three countries has seriously thought about, much less tried to deal with, the structural problems of urban poverty and underemployment (see chapters on Venezuela and Colombia, in Hammergren, 1983).

By what mechanisms have the cooperating elites maintained these liberal democratic regimes and endowed them with legitimacy? Fundamentally, they have replaced the old, highly visible party or personal hegemonies by a much more subtle and flexible joint hegemony of elites who quietly cooperate on the big issues while publicly competing with each other on the smaller issues. Major issues, such as socialism, are not raised or are raised only rhetorically, while most public disputation focuses on narrower—or even totally illusory—points of difference (for example, allegations of government corruption or inefficiency). The electorate thus has the opportunity to vote in honest elections in which a real choice is made between competing parties and candidates. The fact that the opposition candidate often wins the presidency and that majority control of Congress may also shift is a message to the people that they are living in a democracy and that their vote counts. The choice is real, and the popular vote determines the government, but the range of options from which they may choose is limited.

The high-level reality of elite accommodation is further masked by the daily reality of political conflict. The mass media are filled with reports of partisan battles and disputes between organized interests over the details of public policy. It is difficult to see that the objects of conflict, so loudly proclaimed, are less important than the areas of agreement between the antagonists. The daily political spectacle absorbs and entertains as it highlights alternative personalities and marginal issues.

It is not uncommon, of course, for people to realize what is happening, to perceive accurately the degree of elite power prevalent in each system. Even then, though, it is difficult for the citizen to know what else might be done. Accepted ideas and courses of action are so strong that they make alternatives appear quixotic. The bipolar party systems are essential components of this structure in each of the polities we have studied.

The ideological and policy centrism of the party systems is a consequence of the elite accommodation, which presses the competing parties to avoid positions that would be threatening to established interests. In addition, centrism is a direct, strategic response of the parties to the need to build an electoral majority in the context of the winner-take-all character of a strongly presidential political system. The mechanism in each case has been approximately as follows:

1. Democratization of a president-centered political system requires parties to seek an electoral majority in order to win the presidency.
2. Operating from the narrow ground of elite accommodation that makes possible the establishment of democracy, the competing parties progressively socialize the electorate to accept and expect political alternatives from within a narrow range, a range which becomes defined as the "Center."
3. The parties are in turn constrained to stay within the Center thus created, because that is where the voters are.

Thus, the serious presentation of ideological and policy alternatives is discouraged. Similarly, the need for an electoral majority discourages class-based parties, because no single economic class constitutes a majority of the electorate. There is, rather, a premium on multiclass coalitions, the formation of which demands a deemphasis of class conflict.

Alternative viewpoints remain marginal because they are denied the possibility of gaining mass support. They cannot get mass support because no one will take them seriously because they have no mass support. This is true even when minority and dissident groups are tolerated and permitted to articulate their views and seek elective office, as is generally the case at present. Communists and other dissidents have at times been outlawed in all three countries, which obviously makes it even harder to attract mass support. But when participation in the legal political system is open to such a group (for example, MAS in Venezuela), it has two options, neither very promising in the short run.

The first option is to participate in the political system. This holds the long-run possibility of gradually attracting electoral support by making the party's positions known and respectable to the public. In the event of a crisis in one of the dominant parties, then, the dissident party might be in position to become a majority party. In the short run, however, the dissident party's participation in the political process and its token presence in the legislature serve to legitimate the very system it seeks to change, while it can hope to have little, if any, impact on policy.

The other option is scarcely more attractive. If dissidents choose—or are forced into—insurgency against a functioning liberal democratic system, they are likely to find themselves morally and politically isolated and militarily vulnerable. If the regime is working in more or less the manner described above, then it has successfully draped itself in the mantle of popular consent. The insurgents have the unenviable task of convincing people that the government for which they voted is not really their government, that, on the contrary, this group of self-appointed rebels is the legitimate government. It is far easier for insurgents to appeal to people suffering under an open dictatorship than to the voting citizens of the masked hegemony we call liberal democracy.

In such a situation repressive measures often have popular support. The Venezuelan governments of Betancourt and Leoni (AD) repressed the insurgents of the 1960s quite severely, leaving them receptive to the amnesty and legalization offered by Caldera after 1969. A similar situation seems to be evolving in Colombia now. The successive Liberal governments of López Michelsen and Turbay have given the army free rein for counterinsurgency activities against various groups, some of which have shown a willingness to lay down their arms in return for a blanket amnesty and legalization. Turbay was not willing to go that far (some say the army would not permit it), but the Conservative government of Betancur has gone some distance in that direction.

In Costa Rica only a few small groups to the left of the Communists have engaged in violence against the government since 1949. Since 1970 the Communists and other elements of the "mainstream Left" have moved from pacific "quasi illegality" (permitted to exist organizationally, but not to run for office) directly into full participation in party and electoral politics. As for the small numbers of leftists who do engage in political violence, the lightly armed Costa Rican state still seems to have sufficient capabilities in intelligence and repression to keep the "problem" from getting out of hand. But the Costa Rican leadership and press are almost obsessive about such threats to the stability of their society; hence, should the threat become much more serious, a turn to a more repressive regime is not inconceivable. This is one danger in the Costa Rican involvement with anti-Sandinista Nicaraguan groups, which could undermine its political stability.

Other forms of autonomous political organization not controlled by mainstream political forces also tend to be marginalized. Of particular importance here are community organizations of the urban and rural poor, dedicated to land occupation, self-help, community development, or the extraction of resources from the government. Many such groups are entirely spontaneous, while others have been midwifed by Catholic, Protestant, or secular community-development workers. Regardless of their origin, unless they have been promoted by the state bureaucracy itself or by one of the established political forces, the best they can generally expect is to be ignored; the worst is to be destroyed. Pluralism is mainly for the privileged.[7]

Legitimacy for the liberal democratic systems is obtained in part, then, by masking hegemony in pluralist, competitive, strongly centrist political processes. But legitimacy has also followed from the performance of the systems. In Latin America, it is normal for governments to be corrupt, inefficient, and prone to violent political conflict and largely to ignore the welfare of the poor majority. Our three liberal democracies have performed much better than average on both scores. The ameliorative social reforms, while in no way challenging the basic power structure, have provided the less advantaged sectors with some highly visible benefits. And if the spread between rich and poor has not diminished, the standard of living of the majority of the population has improved in very visible ways, such as access to television. In short, the maintenance of the liberal democratic regimes has probably been assisted by their ability to channel sufficient material benefits to the population to stave off desperation. Given the risks and uncertainties of rebellion, most people would have to be more than merely dissatisfied before they would revolt.

Our three liberal democracies have also been characterized by considerably more personal security against political violence than is the norm in Latin America. Since the late 1960s military dictatorships that as a matter of policy carry out large-scale murders and disappearances of their own citizens have been prevalent in the region. In such a context, a liberal democracy that avoids these excesses must look better even to citizens who disagree with its policies. Governments of all three liberal democracies have committed some tragic violations of citizen and human rights, but the scale is minuscule compared with occurrences in Guatemala, Argentina, or Chile. Most of their citizens may be expected to see and appreciate the difference. In Latin America today, the government that does not murder large numbers of its citizens is performing relatively well.

Aspects of the international environment which are virtually uncontrollable by any Latin American country have certainly had a bearing on the maintenance of liberal democracy, but have probably been less critical to the maintenance than to the establishment of the regimes. For example, all three liberal democracies have endured a series of world economic crises since their establishment (the present one being the most serious), but have so far been able to weather the storms. Similarly, there has been at various times an international environment favorable to the emergence of revolutionary insurgencies. The Venezuelan regime defeated its most serious threat and forced it into legal channels. The Colombian regime seems to be moving in the same direction. And the Costa Rican regime, even in turbulent Central America, has thus far averted even the emergence of a serious insurgency.

Finally, there is the matter of United States policy in the region, and that, too, does not seem to have affected our three cases as much as it has some other Latin American countries. American administrations have varied widely in their commitment to promoting human rights and democracy in Latin America; they have varied in the amount and type of aid they were willing to commit to the region; and they have varied in how they expected Latin America to relate to the strategic rivalry with the Soviet Union. The regimes most affected by these changes of policy have been the dictatorships, which have had to endure sudden shifts from warmth to frigidity and back again in their relations with Washington. Yet even the Reagan administration, as friendly as it is with many of the authoritarian regimes in the hemisphere, continues to regard Colombia, Costa Rica, and Venezuela as friends and has shown an active interest in shoring up the regime of Costa Rica in the face of a severe economic crisis. Washington has not always promoted the establishment of liberal democracies, but its support for such regimes once established has been much more general (Schoultz, 1981).

The cases in which the United States has not supported an established democracy are instructive. The major instances are Guatemala (1954; see Immerman, 1982), the Dominican Republic (1965; see Wiarda and Kryzanek, 1982), and Chile (1973; see U.S. Senate Staff Study, 1975). In each case there was the perception that democratic processes had led—or might lead—to a Communist government. In each such case the U.S. government arranged the destruction of the democratic regime.

Colombia, Costa Rica, and Venezuela have never given Washington cause to worry. The explicit elite accommodations upon which their regimes are founded define and maintain dominant political centers that marginalize the radical Left. Here is the main international influence on the maintenance of liberal democracy in these three countries. The elites who have collaborated to form and maintain these regimes cannot have failed to note these effective boundaries of political acceptability, laid down not very tacitly by the dominant power of the hemisphere. They have adapted well.

Liberal democracy in these three cases has been established and maintained in spite of the persistence of profound economic and social inequalities, and there seems to be nothing inherent in liberal democracy that requires serious efforts to reduce or eliminate such inequalities. Each of the three regimes may be seen as a masked hegemony by competing elites who have explicitly agreed to respect one another's vital interests. This masked hegemony is legitimated partially by performance and partially by a political process that is formally democratic, open to any citizen, and under the control of no one political force. The day-to-day reality of dramatic political conflict in such a system masks a fundamental agreement on the acceptable range of public policies. In each case this accepted range of public policies has excluded measures that might be seen by Washington as communistic, thereby averting the possibility of destabilizing intervention by the United States.

## Conclusions: Pluralism and Policy Paralysis

Accommodation between competing elites has been patently successful in maintaining the stability of liberal democracy under the circumstances confronted by contemporary Colombia, Costa Rica, and Venezuela, but their very success holds the seeds of trouble if those circumstances should change. We have seen how difficult it is to break the complex pluralist equilibrium that keeps policy within an established mainstream. That is why these regimes are stable. But the equilibrium would likely hold even when conditions called for innovation. Imagine, for example, a worldwide famine which would make it prohibitively expensive or even impossible to import enough food. Would any of these three political systems be able to break itself out of the mold of present, non-food-oriented agricultural policy? Or would those with an interest in continuing subsidies to agricultural exports be able to frustrate any such reorientation? Or suppose that, against all odds, a socialist government received a clear popular mandate. Would it be able to implement its program any more successfully than did Unidad Popular in Chile?

We have seen that these liberal democracies are masked hegemonies whose very liberalism and pluralism reinforces their stability. But suppose the electorate came to demand more political democratization and economic equalization than the mainstream would normally allow. Could the system respond? How could circumstances be structured so that an appropriate, adaptive response would be forthcoming? How could liberal democracy be transformed into a more meaningful democracy? These are questions of the strategy of change, with which the concluding chapter will concern itself.

# 4

*Maintenance and Beyond: Protection and Democratization of Democracy*

## Inhospitable Soil

THERE IS little reason to think that liberal democratic regimes should take firm root in Latin America. Véliz (1980) has elegantly supported the view that the dominant tradition in the region is centralist, antiliberal, and—a fortiori—antidemocratic. Wiarda (1980) has forcefully argued a similar position, going so far as to suggest that "the use of the 'democratic' label implies not just political and economic imperialism but cultural imperialism as well. Is it not the ultimate in arrogance that we should presume to judge Latin America not by its values but by our own?" (P. 18.)

The argument is compelling if one looks at the whole sweep of Latin American history, for in spite of the repeatedly stated adherence to liberal (and, later, democratic) values, the establishment and persistence of such regimes has been precarious and episodic. We certainly should not assume that all aspects of our own culture are superior to those of Latin America, but the security of the person from violence or death at the hands of the government is a value that transcends cultures.

Who defines a culture, and who benefits from it? Any society is built around a structure of domination in which culture tends to serve the interests of the dominant, but Latin America is heir to a peculiarly direct and violent tradition of domination based on subjugation of indigenous peoples by Iberians intent on extracting wealth from them as rapidly as possible. It simply does not make sense to assume that the predominant values and practices of Latin American civilization represent the interests or desires of anyone other than the ruling classes. When, against the odds, liberal democracy does take root in Latin America, we likewise need not assume that it is an alien import, contrary to the interests or desires of the people.

Wiarda holds that democracy in Latin America should be seen as functioning according to norms that better fit the distinctive cultural context. These norms recognize the

TABLE 7

*Regime Classifications of Howard J. Wiarda*
*(as of 27 January 1978)*

| Democratic | Mixed and Marginal | Authoritarian and Dictatorial | Pariah States |
|---|---|---|---|
| Costa Rica | Peru | Argentina | Nicaragua |
| Venezuela | Brazil | Guatemala | Chile |
| Colombia | Bolivia | El Salvador | |
| Dominican | Honduras | Uruguay | |
| Republic | Cuba | Paraguay | |
| Mexico | Ecuador | | |
| | Panama | | |

concern for individual and collective rights that lies at the core of liberal democratic theory, but Wiarda suggests that these rights operate within the limits of government authority. Strong leadership is taken for granted, and checks on its power are likely to be less effective than in a conventional democracy. However, strong leaders can become tyrannical by failing to show due respect for the rights and privileges of citizens. Wiarda argues, though, that rights and privileges in Latin America are defined largely for collectivities rather than for individuals (Wiarda, 1980, p. 285).

Using scales based on his criteria of democracy in the Latin American context, Wiarda arrives at the classifications listed in Table 7. This approach holds important insights for the study of the Latin American political ethos in that it constitutes a plausible statement of the standards for legitimate government in the region in the late twentieth century. But to attempt to redefine democracy in these terms would simply compound the linguistic confusion surrounding that word. For our purposes, it is more useful as a model of Latin American political values, partially consistent with those of liberal democracy. Wiarda helps us to understand why real liberal democracy is so rare and unstable in Latin America. Yet if liberal democracy is anomalous, it has still occurred.

## Liberal Democracy: Explaining the Anomaly

The approach taken here in analyzing the establishment and maintenance of liberal democracy in Costa Rica, Venezuela, and Colombia has been that of political economy, seeking to explain political phenomena as the result of a complex interaction of economic, social, and political forces through time. In general, we have found that economic and social factors have indeed had a conditioning effect on the development and maintenance of liberal democracy. For example, coffee cultivation had a profound impact on the political systems of all three countries: their twentieth-century political evolution cannot be understood without reference to coffee. Yet it is not possible to attribute the same significance to coffee in all three countries. Furthermore, each country has certain unique economic or social traits that are essential to understanding its politics, but which have no ready parallel in the other countries. For Costa Rica, the relative weakness of the landholding elite and the persistence of a class of independent smallholders have had a profound influence on its politics for a long period of time. The unique and multifaceted roles of the Antioqueños in the economic and political evolution of Colombia has been similarly important. And of course modern Venezuela would be quite a different country without petroleum.

Economic and social factors, in short, are indispensable for understanding the politics of each country, but it is not possible to point to any factor or sequence common to all three countries. Moreover, we saw that it is not possible simply on the basis of economic and social factors to explain the emergence of liberal democracy, or its maintenance, in any of the three countries. For that explanation, it has proven necessary to look at more specifically political conditions in each case.

The establishment of liberal democratic regimes in all three cases was made possible by explicit pacts of accommodation between rival elites. In Colombia the leadership of the Liberal and Conservative parties agreed in 1957 to establish the National Front as a means of transition to a full-fledged liberal democracy. Alternation in the presidency and parity in other offices were intended to allow each party to share in power and to give each a veto over policies threatening to vital interests, thereby eliminating much of the impetus to the partisan violence that had scourged Colombia in the preceding decade. Other key institutions were also part of the accommodation. The church, long a stalwart in the Conservative ranks, accepted the desirability of liberal democracy and the necessity of collaboration with the Liberals. The armed forces, burned by the failure of the Rojas Pinilla dictatorship, were glad to see the traditional parties swallow their differences and resume control of the political system. The leaders of the economy, closely tied to the parties in any case, were similarly happy to see a return to a stable and civilian government. All these sectors supported the Front on the understanding that their vital interests would be respected. The minor parties, the leftist opposition, and the unorganized or inactive sectors of the population were not parties to the accommodation, but their participation was not necessary to its success. The National Front successfully made the transition in 1974 to a fully competitive liberal democracy, though the three presidential elections held since that year are not thought sufficient to warrant judging the Colombian liberal democracy *stable* as yet.

In Venezuela during 1957 political parties that had been at each other's throats during the Trienio of 1945–48 collaborated in the underground within the country, working to overthrow Pérez Jiménez, while abroad the exiled leaders forged an accommodation which lacked the formality of the

National Front but which laid the basis for the establishment of liberal democracy. The leaders of the three main centrist parties at first sought to present a common presidential candidate; when that proved impossible, they did agree to form a grand coalition in support of the victorious presidential candidate. Such an agreement could only have been possible if the parties had moved away from the sectarianism of the Trienio, so that they could give plausible assurances that none would seek to monopolize power at the expense of the others.

As in Colombia, a viable accommodation required the adherence of other key interests besides the parties. The church was not as strong in Venezuela as in Colombia, but the road to liberal democracy was smoothed when the AD leadership convinced the hierarchy that a government led by AD would not be hostile to the church. The armed forces, as in Colombia, were embarrassed by the dictatorship imposed in their name and thus supported the move to restore a liberal democratic regime. The business sector was a particular problem in Venezuela because its leading elements had supported the post-Gómez establishment overthrown in 1945; most business leaders still harbored great distrust and dislike for AD. But the AD leadership made a special point of cultivating this group and assuring them that there would be no renewal of the radical social reformism of the Trienio. Thus assured, most business interests supported the establishment of liberal democracy, though they remained skeptical of AD for some time to come. The victims of this centrist accommodation were the leftist activists of all parties who had collaborated in the underground struggle. It soon became apparent to them that the radical changes that they sought had been sacrificed on the altar of accommodation. Ruthlessly excluded from the centers of power, they rebelled and were thwarted in the mid-1960s.

The victory in 1948 of José Figueres's Army of National Liberation led by a complex route to the successful establishment of a liberal democracy in Costa Rica. First, Figueres signed an agreement with Otilio Ulate (on behalf of whose defrauded candidacy Figueres's forces had fought) which assured Ulate a full term as president after a provisional government led by Figueres decreed certain democratizing changes and oversaw the adoption of a new constitution. When Ulate's party dominated the Constituent Assembly elections and rejected the Social Democratic draft in favor of much more modest changes in the old liberal constitution, Figueres's junta accepted its defeat and handed over power as agreed.

The liberal democracy thus founded initially excluded the defeated parties of 1948, the *calderonistas* and the Communists. The former group had accepted the liberal democratic regime and was active in the partisan political process within the decade, but the latter remained constitutionally excluded for much longer. Of course, the armed forces were defeated and then abolished, and were thus not an interest needing attention as the regime was established. The church hierarchy, formerly allied with Calderón, had to be convinced that the Social Democrats would not press too hard on some of the more anticlerical aspects of their program; they then supported the new regime. Business interests were rather closely allied to Ulate's Unión Nacional and to the other conservative party that had opposed Calderón, the Partido Demócrata. Thus their interests were served by Ulate's control of the Constituent Assembly, which guaranteed a constitutional structure that would protect the privileges of property. Thus, as in the other two cases, the establishment of liberal democracy in Costa Rica was closely wrapped up with the explicit protection of partisan and institutional interests.

These liberal democracies owe their maintenance in large part to a continuation of this same spirit of accommodation between key political sectors.[1] Again, this is easiest to see in the Colombian case, where, in the wake of the resumption of party competition in 1974, an explicit norm has been retained which calls for including members of the opposition party in the cabinet and in other appointive positions. Thus some of the spirit of power-sharing that characterized the National Front remains, reflecting the continued perception of the elites of the two parties that they are jointly responsible for the political system. Moreover, the public discourse of Colombian politics reveals a continuing awareness, rooted in the experiences of La Violencia and the National Front, that liberal democracy can be maintained only if it is actively tended. The other interests whose cooperation was essential to the establishment of the regime have remained in support of it: the church, the armed forces, business. Since 1974, antisystem opposition parties (primarily ANAPO and the Left) have been tolerated, but have not been able to break the basic dominance of the two traditional parties. Various insurgent groups have survived, but have been similarly frustrated; at this writing, some seem headed toward accepting the amnesty and legalization extended to them by the government of President Betancur. Liberal democracy in Colombia is a finely tuned mechanism, assiduously tended by those who operate it, in order to keep it working and to maintain their control of it.

Especially since 1973, the Venezuelan liberal democracy has been dominated by AD and COPEI, while other parties of right, center, and left have been reduced to virtual impotence. What is particularly striking in the context of this discussion is that since 1957 the two parties have built on the accommodation which led to the founding of the liberal democracy. Support for the Venezuelan regime in the 1980s by the leadership of the two parties is fully as self-conscious as it was in the formative stages of the regime. There is, as in Colombia, the sense that they are jointly responsible for the maintenance of the system. But unlike Colombia, there has not been a bipartisan coalition cabinet since the inauguration of President Leoni (1964). Political participation levels are much higher in Venezuela than in Colombia, and political campaigns are spectacularly fought. Yet there remains an awareness that the liberal democratic system must be maintained and the opposition party respected, lest the old days of sectarianism and dictatorship return. Moreover, the coalition supporting liberal democracy has been strengthened by the progressive elimination of *golpista* (procoup) elements in the military, by continued solicitude for the interests of the church, and by steadily growing business support for the regime and for the two main parties. The frustration of the insurgency of the 1960s led to Caldera's amnesty and to the legalization and absorption of the Left into the liberal democratic system. The system thus continues to be consciously supported and legitimated by a wide range of forces whose vital interests are thereby protected.

Like that of Venezuela, the Costa Rican regime has been characterized since its inception by intense competition, in this case between the PLN and shifting opposition coalitions, with neither side able to monopolize the presidency for more than two successive terms. As in Venezuela, political campaigns are intense and dramatic. Yet, building on the long tradition that regards Costa Rica as a uniquely peaceful and civil country within Central America, a strong sense of community has evolved among the political leadership. What started out as an agreement between Figueres and Ulate has been broadened and institutionalized as a commitment to the maintenance of liberal democracy, which is seen in public political discourse virtually as a national treasure. It has not been hard for Costa Ricans to come to see their political system in this light, when they need only look northward to see the travails of their neighbors.

The confidence of rival elites in the system has grown with each election, at least until the recent economic crisis. The base of support for the system has expanded as well, first, to include the *calderonistas* and, more recently and tentatively, the Left. The church, a traditional ally of the *calderonistas*, and the business community, long associated with Ulate, have both been supportive of the regime. The civilian bureaucracy in its present incarnation tends to be *liberacionista*, while the loyalty of the Civil Guard is assured by its partisan membership and military weakness. Each of these last groups can thus also be counted on to support the regime. The rivals may be intensely critical of one another, and indeed of the injustices of Costa Rican society. Not only is the liberal democratic regime itself virtually immune from criticism, but its health and prospects are discussed constantly in the press and in public pronouncements of elites. Rather than take the persistence of the regime for granted, the elites assume that it is precarious, and acknowledge their responsibility to concern themselves with its maintenance.

## The Importance of Political Choice

This emphasis on the critical role of elite accommodation in the foundation and maintenance of liberal democracy is consistent with a broad trend in political science during the last decade. The trend is a renewed emphasis on political choice, or the autonomy of political actors. Almond, Flanagan, and Mundt (1973) sought to develop a model, based on case studies, of the interaction between environmental determinants and the choices of political leaders, with particular attention to crisis situations. Linz and Stepan (1978) argued that the breakdown of democratic regimes could be substantially explained in a large number of cases on the basis of specific choices and interactions of political leaders; the social and economic environment was again interpreted not as determinative, but rather as setting boundaries for action. Nordlinger (1981) developed and defended the proposition that, far from being controlled by its social environment, the state in modern democracies in fact exercises considerable autonomy in policy and program.

The recognition of the partial autonomy of political actors, relative to their social and economic environments, has been characteristic of much of the best recent Marxian scholarship. Nicos Poulantzas (1978) sought to develop a comprehensive theory of the state in advanced capitalism, in which the political processes of liberal democracy were seen as having considerable autonomy, relative to structures of class domination. E. P. Thompson (1978) has strongly rejected the reifications of an unduly deterministic Marxism, affirming instead the capacity and obligation of political actors to transform reality by their actions. Finally, the dissident school of humanistic Marxists, exemplified by Markovic (1982), seeks to break with the bureaucratic and deterministic orthodoxies of Soviet Marxism in order to reemphasize Marx's call for coupling theoretical understanding with creative action.

Elite accommodation is, of course, the type of autonomous political action in question here, and it calls to mind the growing literature on consociational democracy. One of the leading exponents of that concept, Arend Lijphart, has defined consociational democracy as a type of democracy that responds to the conditions of "plural society," in which parties and other politically relevant divisions coincide with religious, ideological, ethnic, or other deeply felt social cleavages (see Eckstein, 1966, p. 34). Within such a plural society, democratic practices and political stability can be maintained through consociational mechanisms. Four characteristics serve to define the phenomenon. First, a grand coalition is formed, including the leaders of all significant segments of the society. Second, the interests of each segment are protected by conceding it a veto on policy issues vital to it. Third, representation in political and governmental office is proportionate to the strength of the segment. Finally, each segment has great autonomy for its internal affairs (Lijphart, 1977, p. 25). In effect, consociational democracy is an arrangement to circumscribe majority rule in order to protect the rights of multiple minorities. On the basis that they do not qualify as plural societies, then, Lijphart excludes both Colombia and Uruguay as consociational democracies (1977, pp. 33, 212ff.), though he acknowledges that both have used some consociational mechanisms.

Dix (1980) has held that Colombia should be regarded as a consociational democracy, that the partisan cleavage is so deep and durable as to make the competing groups the functional equivalent of subcultures. There is, of course, no doubt that the institutional arrangements of the National Front fit the consociational model. Dix further argues that the factors cited by Lijphart as likely to facilitate the success of consociationalism are of little use in understanding the Colombian case. Rather than look at relatively constant structural conditions that may make consociational democracy possible (for example, a pattern of limited contact between the subcultures), Dix suggests that it is more useful to look at *changing* circumstances which explain changes in elite behavior. As he puts it, the question is, Why now but not before? (p. 132).

Dix's case for calling the Colombian National Front a consociational regime is compelling. The same cannot be said for the post-1974 Colombian regime or for the liberal democracies of Costa Rica and Venezuela. These latter cases seem to fit much better the pluralist model embodied in Dahl's concept of polyarchy (compare Dahl, 1971). That is, there are few *formal* restrictions on political competition and conflict or on the exercise of majority rule through elections and representative institutions. This study, however, has shown that there are a great many explicit but informal restrictions on competition and majority rule in all three countries. So if we are not, strictly speaking, dealing in these cases with consociational democracy, we are dealing with regimes based on elite accommodation, as a means of reducing destructive political tensions. We are dealing, in short, with political choice, where other choices might have been made. That this is consistent with contemporary comparative scholarship on democratic regimes is attested to by the following passage from the recent comprehensive study of G. Bingham Powell (1982, p. 226; compare Lijphart, 1984):

There are many ways to organize a working democracy. The different approaches tend to have different advantages and disadvantages. The implications of a given approach depend in part on what sorts of performance are most strongly desired. Creative political leadership can help to mitigate the undesirable qualities, or undermine the benefits, in any type of setting. It is important not to draw too sweeping inferences about the effects of proportional representation, or political extremism, or citizen participation from their presence in one particular country or another.

## The Experience of Democracy in Latin America

In this cautious spirit, on the basis of our three cases it is possible to set forth a tentative hypothesis that an ongoing spirit of elite accommodation is requisite to the establishment and maintenance of liberal democracy in Latin America. All but the most backward countries in the region have experienced more than one attempt to establish a liberal regime in this century (compare Wesson, 1982). Most such enterprises have lasted less than one presidential term, ending, typically, in a military coup supported by the opposition. The establishment of liberal democracy is a normal part of the political cycle in most Latin American countries, but few such regimes persist. The findings of this study suggest that Latin American liberal democracies founded without an explicit accommodation between key elites are extremely unlikely to survive. A review of major cases of abortive or unstable democratic regimes supports the argument (good summaries are contained in Wiarda and Kline, 1979, and Peeler, 1983).

The regime established in 1965 in the Dominican Republic, on the points of U.S. bayonets, was an inauspicious beginning for a liberal democracy. Juan Bosch and his Partido Revolucionario (PR) were excluded from the political arena, while elements of the old Trujillo elite took the reins of power under the elected presidency of Joaquín Balaguer. Yet a decade later, when Balaguer retired, honest elections were held and Balaguer peacefully handed over power to a much more moderate PR (without Bosch). Honest elections were again held in 1980, and the PR candidate won again. This time, however, the Carter Administration had to help dissuade elements of the armed forces from a planned preemptive coup in order to allow the new government to take office as scheduled. Thus it is too soon to say that the liberal democracy of the Dominican Republic has achieved stability, but formerly hostile elites have moved closer to the requisite accommodation than anywhere else in the region.

By contrast, the Andean states of Peru, Ecuador, and Bolivia have seen repeated unsuccessful attempts in the last generation to constitute liberal democratic regimes. All are today governed by elected civilian presidents under liberal democratic constitutional regimes, but it would be surprising if all three regimes survived unbroken through 1985. In these countries whether an elite supports liberal democracy depends on whether it supports the particular government in power. Opponents of the government oppose the liberal democratic regime and are willing to accept—sometimes to encourage—a military coup to remove that government. There are obviously major differences between these three countries, but with respect to the stability of liberal democracy, they are in similar situations. In the absence of accommodation between rival civilian elites, the armed forces retain the opportunity to intervene periodically (Finer, 1975).

Since 1930 Argentina has been widely viewed as an anomaly because of the persistent juxtaposition of a high level of economic development with political instability. Huntington (1968) used Argentina as his major example of a "mass praetorian" society, that is, one characterized by political institutions unable to control very high levels of mass political mobilization. O'Donnell (1979) built upon this conceptual scheme to formulate his model of the "bureaucratic-authoritarian regime," in which a coalition of military bureaucrats and civilian bureaucrats, supported by the bourgeoisie, seizes power. They set up an authoritarian regime with the purpose of forcing the political demobilization of the working masses in order to clear the way for economic "rationalization." O'Donnell uses Argentina and Brazil as his primary examples of such a regime. Since O'Donnell first wrote (1973), in fact, the first bureaucratic-authoritarian regime (1966–73) made way for the return of Juan Peron, whose widow was in turn removed by the military in 1976, when a new military regime was set up. Its savage repressiveness (thousands of disappeared persons, for example), along with the patent failure of its economic program, led to such popular unrest that the regime desperately attempted the seizure of the Malvinas in 1982 in order to distract the public from their grievances. The resulting military debacle left not only the regime but the armed forces as a whole profoundly weakened and discredited (Cavarozzi, 1982).

Demoralized, the top officers could only fume impotently as a rising wave of protest enveloped the country, protest directed not only at the humiliation in the Malvinas but also increasingly at the regime's repressiveness and economic incompetence. Heads began to roll among the top military leadership, and free elections were set for late 1983. The transitional junta presided over by Gen. Reinaldo Bignone decreed an amnesty for military officers accused of crimes committed under the post-1976 regime, but civilians of virtually all political sectors denied the amnesty's validity. When the elections led to a decisive victory by the Radical nominee, Raúl Alfonsín, over the Peronist candidate, the sorry remnants of the military government were so anxious to leave that they voluntarily advanced the inauguration date by two months. Alfonsín was inaugurated in December 1983. Will this transition to democracy prove to be the beginning of a stable regime? One critical consideration is whether the main partisan rivals, the Radicals and the

Peronists, will come to see a joint stake in maintaining a democratic regime, rather than in fighting political wars that will paralyze the government and, ultimately, draw the armed forces back into the arena.

It probably strikes some readers as more than odd that nothing has been said in this book about Mexico as a democracy. That is because it is not one. But Mexico does represent a successful institutionalization and liberalization of the traditional Latin American hegemony. Since Calles founded the Revolutionary party in 1928, the personal authority of the *caudillo* president has been transmuted into the institutional authority of the party's designee, who holds virtually dictatorial powers for six years, selects his successor (after elaborate consultations), and retires. The institutional party functions much like the personal following of a *caudillo*, save that the party automatically transfers its allegiance from one president to the next. Thus the great weakness of *caudillismo*, the necessity to remove incumbents by force, has been solved. Very much in the tradition of *caudillismo*, elections are held regularly—and are almost always won by the Partido Revolucionario Institucional. Fraud, however, is seldom a necessity anymore because the party's predominance is so institutionalized.

In order to legitimize its hegemony, the revolutionary establishment has shaped a substantially liberal political system in which the opposition is free to organize and compete and citizens have not only the right to vote but also substantial civil liberties. Since only one candidate has a chance of winning in any given election, however, Mexico cannot be called a liberal democracy. Accommodation between rival elites has not been necessary to assure political stability in Mexico because one elite coalition virtually monopolizes power. Still, the liberalization of the Mexican political system is an accommodation on the part of the dominant elite, allowing a degree of freedom and consideration for their opponents beyond what they would have to concede.

For at least a decade the bureaucratic-authoritarian regime of Brazil has been seeking to institutionalize a controlled liberal regime reminiscent of the Mexican system, but with the dominant party being affiliated with the conservative armed forces. This does not seem to be working, if one can judge by the antiregime victories in the 1982 elections. The regime may have to choose between a return to a more overtly oppressive policy and handing over power to elements of the opposition. If the latter occurs, both regime and opposition will have to decide whether to seek the sort of accommodation which could lay the basis for a stable liberal democracy.

Could it be that the fragility of democracy in these cases is partially attributable to the attempt to superimpose it on an elite political culture notably lacking in a spirit of accommodation? As Véliz would remind us, there is little in the Iberian centralist tradition to encourage an incumbent ruler voluntarily to surrender power to his opponents; conversely, there is little reason for opponents to trust any means but force for the removal of an incumbent. And even if the incumbent respects the limits suggested by Wiarda (see above), his opponents must either come to terms with him or seek to remove him, unless they wish to resign themselves to a perpetually disadvantaged situation. If the incumbent does not respect those limits, his opponents may expect violent repression, and would be justified, under Wiarda's scheme, in seeking his overthrow. In a game with such rules, it would be irrational—if not indeed insane—for a ruler to hold honest elections and surrender power to his opponents; it would be similarly foolhardy for opponents to put their trust in constitutional guarantees and electoral probity. In such systems, liberal democracy is simply a normal passing phase in a recurring political cycle.

The establishment of stable liberal democracy in the three cases we have studied then appears as a fundamental change in the rules of the game. Elites who had played by the rules sketched out in the preceding paragraph were able to convince one another that, regardless of who won elections and who held power, their opponents might reasonably hope for victory another time, and would not in the interim be oppressed. From being a phase in the cycle of the normal Latin American political system, liberal democracy becomes the context of the political cycle. From being an instrument for the hegemony of one political force over others, liberal democracy becomes a framework for the shared hegemony of rival forces.

Even after its establishment as a stable regime, however, liberal democracy is less secure in the countries of Latin America than in the North Atlantic area. The breakdown of liberal democracy in Uruguay and Chile is instructive.[2] Uruguay provides a particularly clear case of a long tradition of accommodation between rival elites; the country experimented for two sustained periods with a collegial executive guaranteeing representation to both traditional parties. There was clearly an awareness among the traditional party elites that they had to accommodate one another's interests or risk civil war. But the system of centrist accommodation proved too fragile to cope with a determined leftist insurgency and the resultant rightist demand for order at all costs. In 1973 the civilian president submitted to the de facto control of the armed forces, and the Uruguayan democracy died.

Chile's democratic regime appears to have had very little tradition of explicit elite accommodation: those who held power were not expected to refrain from pursuing their interests as far as they were able. The norm of electoral honesty, however, was very strong, constituting an important safeguard for opposition interests. Further, the checks and balances of the Chilean constitution virtually assured that no government could control all levers of power; thus radical departures in policy could be frustrated or diluted. From the mid-1930s until the early 1970s, this procedurally balanced structure permitted serious democratic competition between class-based and ideological parties covering a much broader spectrum than any of the other Latin American democracies have been able to countenance. In the Chilean case, procedure would seem to have been a strong enough norm to stabilize the system for nearly forty years, even in the absence of explicit accommodation between rival elites with fundamentally conflicting interests.

In the 1960s, though, endogenous and exogenous strains began to affect the system. The electoral strength of the Left led to the initiation of a program of covert intervention by the United States (U.S. Senate Staff Study, 1975), while the relative absence of trust between rival elites may have made them more receptive to such outside help as a means of frustrating their opponents. Valenzuela (1978, p. xiii) has argued that the rise of the Christian Democrats to dominance in the mid-1960s contributed to the breakdown of democracy because of the determination of that party to abstain from any alliances with other parties. Of course it is well known that United States intervention assisted the Christian Democrats in gaining that position of dominance. The failure of the Christian Democrats and the Right to cooperate led to Allende's minority victory in the presidential election of 1970. From 1970 to 1973 the rejection of accommodation progressively wrecked the procedural balance of the constitutional system. The intransigence of the Far Left and Far Right in rejecting any compromise led to polarization and the escalation of violence. Finally, the Center and Right virtually invited a military coup, as preferable to the continuation of the Left in office.

These two cases of democratic breakdown embody quite different lessons. Uruguay represents the failure of accommodation under pressure from right and left. The Chilean case shows a system torn apart because the forces dominating it could not accept control of the presidency by advocates of radical change whose participation in the political process had long been tolerated. Chile is an example of what can happen to a liberal democracy under stress, given a weak tradition of accommodation. Uruguay shows us that accommodation only works within a particular range of political forces and policy options. Certainly none of our three cases is immune from such breakdowns, though this does not seem imminent in any of them. The fact that liberal democracy could so quickly unravel even in long-established regimes like Chile and Uruguay simply serves to reemphasize the remarkable, anomalous character of the three liberal democracies we have studied. Few Latin American elites have taken and sustained the choice of accommodation. For those who have, the consequences have been important.

## The Consequences of Accommodation

Structurally, accommodation between rival elites has had the obvious effect of bolstering the institutions of liberal democracy. Concretely, that means (among other things) strengthening the tendency to immobilism that is inherent in liberal institutions. Limitations on governmental authority, protection of individual rights, constitutional checks and balances—all serve to make it harder for any government to decide and act upon major departures in policy. Moreover, the natural tendency of these presidential systems to evolve toward bipolar party systems has promoted the well-known centrist dynamic (discussed in chapter 3), whereby parties seek the center because the voters are there, while voters consider voting only for the center parties because everyone else votes for them, making them the only parties with a chance to win. Such a party system discourages parties and candidates from offering new ideas. Finally, multiple organized interests have relatively free play in a liberal democracy, all eager to defend their interests by influencing policy. It is hardly likely in such a setting that a government will break free of all these conflicting pressures in order to implement a radically innovative policy. Liberal democracy as a structure, in short, tends to lock the choices of policy and leadership into a relatively narrow range around what comes to be called the center of the political spectrum.

This structural centrism has a substantive value content derived from the historical circumstances of liberal democracy as we have known it. The values and interests it tends to protect are those of the already privileged, the local and international operators of firms oriented to international trade, and, more generally, the more affluent and educated sectors of society. Structural immobilism virtually assures these sectors that policies threatening their vital interests will not be implemented. Moreover, the privileged sectors have advantages in material resources, contacts, and organization which enable them to get the most out of the give-and-take of the political process. Since all three of these societies, like the rest of Latin America, are characterized by extreme economic inequality to the point of palpable injustice, then liberal democracy's immobilism must be seen as defending social injustice by making it virtually impossible to bring about fundamental change.

The pacts of accommodation which laid the basis for our three regimes make these systemic tendencies explicit and binding. In addition to guaranteeing that the rival parties will not seek to destroy one another, the fundamental interests of the economic leadership of the country are also assured respect. We have seen the results in the political economy of each of the countries. The state is relatively strong, intervening in the economy for the purpose of enhancing the health of capitalism. The state also administers social service programs which ameliorate the worst effects of injustice and it carries out social and economic reforms (for example, agrarian reform) which again ameliorate injustice without threatening the basic structure of the system. Pressure for radical change is thus eased. Liberal democracy functions as a flexible shield for the economic and social status quo.

## The Worth of Liberal Democracy

If liberal democracy in Latin America, even more than elsewhere, functions to protect and preserve injustice, it is worth asking why we should regard it as valuable. The attainment of liberal democracy is not an end in itself. If a political order were feasible which would better serve the ends of justice, we all, including Latin Americans, would be wise to opt for it. Of all the political systems in Latin America which at the present time are not liberal democracies, however, few by any standard provide more social and economic equality than the three countries we have studied. And it is fair to say that none provides more effective civil and political liberties, including protection from arbitrary imprisonment, torture, and death at the hands of the government. The regimes that replaced liberal democracies in Chile and Uruguay have been among the worst offenders in this respect.

All of the likely alternatives to liberal democracy in Latin America are worse; that is why liberal democracy, if it can be attained, is worth having. This is not the same as saying that justice is unattainable or that revolution is impossible. We should work toward those ends whenever the opportunity presents itself, but we should also recognize that the normal balance of internal and international forces makes a descent into repression far more likely than the successful establishment of a significantly more egalitarian society. In short, we should not be satisfied with liberal democracy, but neither should we idly risk its destruction or denigrate its achievements in a world in which life can be far more brutish.

## Coping with Threats to Liberal Democracy

The main threat to the stable liberal democracies in the current climate of Latin America is from the right, from civilian and military sectors that fear a threat to the economic and political order from continued or accelerated popular political mobilization. In the climate created by the Cold War foreign policies of a succession of United States governments, the natural coloration of this rightist opposition is anti-Communist. As long as the centrist accommodation dominates the scene, the antidemocratic reaction has very little scope for action. But a breakdown in accommodation, or even modest leftist electoral success, could provide an opening for the Right, while even the smallest exploits of a leftist insurgency are enough to provoke truculent outbursts from the Right.

Venezuela dealt successfully with this problem in the 1960s. Though small insurgent groups are still fighting the regime, its stability is not presently in danger. The Left is weaker in Colombia, but its ability to sustain a variety of insurgencies has been more persistent. As a result, in the late 1970s, it was widely thought that Colombia was drifting in the same direction taken by Uruguay, toward a military-dominated bureaucratic-authoritarian regime. By 1982, however, the relative weakness of the insurgents had made some of them more receptive to the amnesty offer of the Betancur government, an offer which was considerably more flexible than that offered by President Turbay. The result is that Colombia may also be on the way to renewed stability for its liberal democracy.

The most vulnerable of the three regimes at present is that of Costa Rica. Its location on the southern border of Nicaragua has given it an unaccustomed prominence in the foreign policy of the Reagan administration, while the profundity of its economic crisis has made it completely vulnerable to U.S. pressures. At the same time that the government is being forced to scale back its social services and reduce the standard of living of the population, it is being pressured to upgrade its military and police capabilities and to turn a blind eye to anti-Sandinista operations launched from Costa Rica. Given these outside pressures and the existence within the country of a strong and vocal right wing (especially the Movimiento Costa Rica Libre), the transformation of the Costa Rican liberal democracy into something on the Uruguayan model is not at all inconceivable in the event of guerrilla or terrorist activity within the country. So far, though, the centrist accommodation has held, and the commitment of the dominant elites to the maintenance of liberal democracy should not be underestimated.

If the centrist elites, whose accommodation has made the system possible in each country, realize the value of the regime and continue to act jointly to maintain it, then its survival against the threat from the right is likely. If the Left also accepts the regime as a good thing in spite of its faults and works within it rather than against it, it will be even harder for the Right to destroy liberal democracy. This puts the Left in the position of supporting and participating in a regime which is structurally and politically biased against it, but this seems the better course because a successful popular revolution against a functioning liberal democracy is far less likely than the provocation of a rightist takeover, with its attendant violent suppression of the Left.

The Right itself should bear in mind that seizure of absolute power carries with it absolute responsibility and blame. The decline and decay of bureaucratic-authoritarian regimes in Argentina, Uruguay, Brazil, and Chile suggest that the final solutions for which the Right so passionately longs are not attainable. With the fall of these regimes, the Right may find itself in far worse straits than before.

Save in cases in which policymakers have perceived (rightly or wrongly) substantial Communist involvement, it has not been United States policy actively to undermine stable liberal democracies. Even the Reagan administration has not sought to do that. In pursuit of strategic ends in a Cold War context, however, the United States may well inadvertently undermine liberal democracies. This is the current danger in Costa Rica. As long as the tragic cycle of hostility with the Soviet Union remains a reality, it is inevitable that a key criterion of U.S. policy will be preventing the emergence of another Soviet ally in Latin America. Since World War II, American policymakers have frequently assumed that any leftist or nationalist regime posed a threat, while overtly anti-Communist, authoritarian regimes have frequently been thought the best bulwarks against Communism. Such assumptions are shortsighted and self-defeating.

An intelligent U.S. foreign policy for Latin America would seek actively to foster and protect liberal democracies because when such regimes are working well, they absorb and muffle mass discontent in relatively harmless ways, rather than leave the discontented available for mobilization by radical dissidents. Moreover, the persistent association of the United States with the most repressive regimes in the hemisphere can only undermine our moral authority as leaders of the "Free World." Further, the United States should accept and work with radical regimes as long as they refrain from alliance with the Soviet Union. The contrary policy, now being pursued against Nicaragua, is having the self-fulfilling effect of pushing the Sandinistas into the arms of the Soviets. Indeed, the United States would be well advised to foster independent radical regimes, since by dealing effectively with such structural problems as the maldistribution of resources, they will enhance the prospects for stability in the long run. But it is more realistic for Latin Americans to assume that any improvements they make in their societies will be over the opposition of the United States.

## *The Establishment of Stable Liberal Democracies Elsewhere in Latin America*

The cases of Colombia, Costa Rica, and Venezuela suggest circumstances in which liberal democracy might be established and maintained elsewhere in Latin America. Most countries in Latin America probably experience on occasion the conditions under which a stable liberal democracy might be established. The lesson of the other cases we have just reviewed is that these conditions are not usually taken advantage of; consequently, liberal democracy remains simply a stage in the normal political cycle, rather than becoming the basis of a stable system.

The policy advocated for the United States in the previous section, to foster and protect liberal democracy, is particularly critical in dealing with countries that have not yet established stable democratic regimes. In dealing with political systems in flux, a North American policy which not only favored the establishment of liberal democracy but actively pressed for the kind of broad accommodation of which we have spoken in this book could yield significant successes in the long run.

Of course, even if we come to the considered judgment that establishing stable liberal democracies is on balance a good idea, we must remember that such a step has costs. Most notably each of the sectors involved must accept that it is not going to dominate the system and that it will have to yield to the vital interests of its opponents if it is to see its own protected. The elites involved will be cognizant of any explicit accommodations, but their mass followings may not be. That potential disjunction poses a serious danger to the elites, as mass sectors may come to feel betrayed by their leaders. Further, the sectors that sacrifice the most for a stable liberal democracy are those that advocate and have a stake in radical change, since liberal democracy is structurally resistant to such change, a resistance strengthened by elite accommodation. Rather than confine themselves within the straitened possibilities of liberal democracy, however safe that may be, then, many radicals may be willing to risk the savage repressiveness of the rightist alternatives in hopes of eventually achieving a successful revolution.

## Democratizing Liberal Democracy

Is it possible to break liberal democracy out of its confining mold and to move toward a fuller democracy without sacrificing liberal virtues? Having seen the structural immobilism of liberal democracy, it should be clear that any sort of fundamental change in such a system will require very special circumstances. Those might include, first, conditions that could make a transition to a more democratic system possible and, second, other conditions that would bring about such a transition.

A situation that could allow for a democratic transition might occur if several circumstances combined to break down the normal structure of domination which supports liberal democracies and other regimes in Latin America. Suppose, for example, that the forces opposed to change were divided by political rivalries. It is not uncommon for parties and organized groups that share substantial interests to be nevertheless unable to work together at a particular time, perhaps because of other interests which conflict, colliding ambitions of the various leaders, or old grudges.

Suppose, furthermore, that the armed forces were divided about their proper political role. Huntington (1957) has argued that it is normal for professional soldiers to be politically conservative, in light of their mission of defending the nation. Whether that is always the case (compare Huntington, 1968), at the present time in Latin America, North American doctrines of national security pervade all military establishments. Those doctrines strongly emphasize the role of the armed forces in defending against internal subversion; such a mission would predispose the military to oppose the Left in national politics. Thus, united armed forces may be expected to resist sweeping democratization of the political system. If an officer corps were divided by conflicting ambition, divergent political views, service rivalries, or disagreements about whether the armed forces should control the government, however, an opening might occur for the implementation of changes that might otherwise be unfeasible.

Suppose, in addition, that the United States followed a policy of nonintervention or of support for human rights. Occasionally a U.S. administration may find itself at odds with one or another reactionary dictatorship in Latin America, and sometimes (as with Wilson, Kennedy, or Carter) one finds an incipient prodemocratic policy, but the overall thrust of the United States in Latin America is unquestionably conservative. Thus anytime a U.S. administration pursues a policy of nonintervention, the forces of change are likely to benefit. And even if it is inconsistently pursued (as with Carter), a policy favoring the defense of human rights will tend to provide the forces demanding change with more space in which to operate safely.

Finally, suppose that interested transnational corporations lacked the full support of the United States government. Traditionally U.S. foreign policy in Latin America defends the interests of American firms doing business in the region, but a given administration need not find this concern compelling in every case. For example, larger strategic considerations might induce Washington to overlook pressure being put on an American firm if the country in question were seen as sufficiently vital. Or support might be withheld simply because the company in question lacked good connections in Washington. In either case, a firm which had been a major bulwark of the status quo could find itself vulnerable.

In such a conjuncture of circumstances a more radical change would become possible. There remains then the question of the conditions that would actually bring about democratizing change. Broadly speaking, we may conceive of four approaches to bringing about such change.

Within a liberal democracy, the most obvious and least disruptive approach is for the advocates of democratizing change to win an election and implement their program. The problem here is that liberal democracy in practice tends to evolve into a highly centrist party system in which advocates of serious change are usually marginalized. In fact, the pacts of accommodation underlying all three of our liberal democracies essentially exclude fundamental changes. The reformism typical of the center-left parties in the liberal democracies thus holds little promise of achieving fundamental change because the reformers' price of entry into the system has been precisely their agreement not to make such changes.

A definitive move in the direction of democratization might still come through elections, though. In circumstances of profound crisis, an electoral realignment might favor the democratizing forces. During the 1930s in Scandinavia, the social democratic parties achieved lasting electoral dominance as a result of voter reaction to the world economic crisis.[3] Social democratic dominance was then cemented by a series of effective governments that carried out their programs while respecting public liberties. In effect, the "center" of the system moved from liberalism to social democracy in the space of a few years. There is no longer a question in Scandinavia of restoring the old liberal political economy; the rightist alternative today is simply not expanding the social democratic system.

On very rare occasions within functioning liberal democracies, conditions may favor a coup directed to breaking the obstacles to further democratization. This strategy is much more appropriate in other types of regimes, but even a liberal democracy sometimes produces an elected government that is blatantly corrupt or incompetent or one that is persistently unresponsive to popular needs in a major economic crisis. The balance of political forces might then permit a successful coup even against a "democratically" elected government whose legitimacy had been undermined. The new provisional regime would then be in a position to sweep aside many of the old centers of power and set up a new constitutional regime built around a new political center. Such a democratizing coup is unlikely to come from the armed forces. For the coup to succeed, the armed forces would have to be split, immobilized, or defeated. This is a major reason why the democratizing coup is not normally practical.

That such a coup could happen, however, is attested to by the crisis of 1948 in Costa Rica, when the irregular Army of National Liberation defeated the government and its army and took power. The political-economic elite was divided and disarmed, the army was defeated, and the United States did not oppose the movement because of its preoccupation with the Communist influence in the previous government. The conjuncture, in short, would have been ideal for the imposition of the democratizing program of the Social Democrats. As we saw, however, what actually happened was the strengthening of liberal democracy through accommodation with conservative interests.

The last approach for democratizing change is full-scale revolution, but this would not be feasible as long as the liberal democracy were functioning well because a revolution requires mass support. The potential mass support for such a movement in a working liberal democracy would already be mobilized by the parties of the center, while the existence of liberal freedoms and party competition would make it harder to convince people that violent opposition was justified. And when a liberal democratic regime breaks down, there are ample historical precedents to suggest that the more likely successor will be reactionary, not revolutionary (namely, Mussolini, Franco, Hitler, and Pinochet). Revolution, like a coup, is a much more viable option against a naked dictatorship than against a working liberal democracy.

It is not surprising that there are no sure and easy paths to the further democratization of liberal democracy. As long as the regime continues to work reasonably well, the two electoral strategies recommend themselves. If the liberal democracy unravels seriously, one of the more violent strategies may become appropriate. If the odds of success are not high in any case, change can and does occur.

In Latin America a critical question is how such a new democratizing regime could keep from being overthrown.

That would depend in part on the persistence of the breakdown in the structure of domination (referred to above) which provided the opening for democratizing change in the first place. For such a regime to be maintained, the opponents of transformation would have to be so weakened that they would be constrained to accept the new political and economic order. And the democratizing leadership would even then be endangered whenever, for example, the policy of the United States became more assertive or conservative.

Any democratizing regime in Latin America is also likely to encounter resistance from reactionary terrorist organizations, which are likely to be active even in the absence of external support from the United States or elsewhere. In societies built on intense exploitation, any attempt to reduce that exploitation will be resisted by those who stand to lose, and in the Latin American context it should not be surprising that some of that resistance will be violent. The key to containing such reactionary violence will lie in its marginalization through the maintenance of popular support for the regime.

The lessons of liberal democracy itself could be important in the struggle to maintain a democratizing regime. It is hard to destabilize a working liberal democracy, hard to introduce radical change into it, because of the checks and balances of pluralism. Moreover, the existence of freedom, competition, and choice within the mainstream of a liberal democracy tends to convince citizens that there is no need or justification for opposition outside that mainstream. Liberal democracy is an ingenious mechanism for the dynamic stabilization of a political system. After it undercut the power base of opponents of democratization, a newly established democratizing regime could fortify itself by reimplanting the centrist and indeed immobilist mechanisms of liberal democracy in order to restrain and marginalize the advocates of reaction.[4] Liberal democracy as a structure has a genius which transcends the defense of capitalism, the role to which it was born.

## Conclusion: Toward a Model of a
## Working Democracy in Latin America

This book has criticized liberal democracy for its immobilism and defense of privilege. On the other hand, Véliz (1980), Wiarda (1980, 1982), and others have criticized liberal democracy as alien to the Iberian cultural tradition. They argue that the emphasis of liberal democracy on inalienable individual rights, limited government, and a political process characterized by pluralistic competition is in conflict with a deeply rooted tradition in Latin America which calls for centralized authority, corporatism, and the subordination of individual interests to the common good. The tendency of democratic theory exemplified by C. B. Macpherson, however, can deal with both sets of objections. Using his formulations, there is the possibility of a more truly democratic regime which nevertheless fits well within the Latin American tradition. To make this point it will first be necessary to consider Macpherson's thought in more detail than has heretofore been necessary.

Macpherson's explicit goal has been to retrieve the end of human liberation from the impasse into which modern liberalism has fallen. Participatory democracy, in his view, is intimately tied up with human liberation. Liberal thinkers (Mill perhaps most systematically) have tried to build a theory of democracy into the basic defense of liberty against government interference that lies at the core of the theory. Macpherson holds that this enterprise could not succeed, because liberals typically have held defective concepts of human nature, liberty, and property. Liberals have conceived of human nature as characterized by what Macpherson has called "possessive individualism": each person is thought of as competing with every other for control over the means of satisfying infinite desires. In liberal thought and practice, this has been taken to mean that no person should deliberately interfere with another's pursuit of utilities, that the acquisition of private property does not of itself constitute such interference with others, and that government should interfere with citizens' liberties only enough to protect property and keep people from violating each other's liberties. It is Macpherson's view that this liberal complex in fact makes impossible the maximization of liberty for all persons because it ignores the inevitable restriction of the possibilities of those who lose out in the competitive struggle.

Macpherson's attempt to renovate liberal democratic theory centers on a radically different concept of human nature, based on Mill's revision of utilitarianism. This is "a view of man's essence not as a consumer of utilities but as a doer, a creator, an enjoyer of his human attributes" (1973, p. 4). His aim is to liberate each individual from impediments to the development of his or her own powers as a human being. The fundamental character of human existence can change, so that people do not have to be simply "maximizers of utilities." What they may become is fundamentally up to each person.

Anytime one person is able to extract benefit from another, the latter is thereby deprived of some part of his or her power to use human capacities for self-development. People must therefore be protected from the extractive power of others, as a prerequisite to the more positive "ability to live in accordance with one's own conscious purposes, to act and decide for oneself rather than to be acted upon and decided for by others" (1973, p. 109). A society maximizes human powers and liberty to the extent that it provides all persons with property, redefined as adequate access to the means of life and the means of labor, and protects them from invasion by other persons. (For a fuller discussion of the concepts of power and liberty presented in this paragraph, see Macpherson, 1973, essays 1, 3, and 5. Compare Berlin, 1969.)

Macpherson is concerned more with a way of life than simply with a form of government, but democratic government is an essential aspect of a democratic society. One connotation of property as access to the means to a fully human life is the right to share in political power. Macpherson's *The Life and Times of Liberal Democracy* (1977) is devoted to showing the necessity of participatory democracy as a means to the human development of citizens, and to sketching the outlines of how we might approach it and how it might work. It is hard to see how a society of possessive individualists would even want to change, much less be able to change, in the direction advocated by Macpherson. His basic strategy is to look for contradictions in the established order that might initiate the dialectical process of cultural and structural change in the direction of a more democratic society.

Macpherson's attempt to reconstitute liberal democratic theory is appealing and indeed compelling, but his greatest difficulty lies precisely at the center of his own reconstruction: the developmental concept of human nature. In trying to escape possessive individualism while also avoiding the dangers of coercion by those who "know the truth," he would proscribe much exploitative behavior prevalent in contemporary society, but the positive content remains minimal.

Although Macpherson directs his reconstitution of democratic thought at the fundamentally liberal polities of the North Atlantic world, his approach would deal with the main problems raised in this book (immobilism and the defense of privilege), and with those raised by Wiarda and others (liberal democracy as inconsistent with the Iberian cultural tradition). The narrowly self-seeking individualism and pluralism characteristic of liberal democracy have been rejected by Macpherson in favor of a conception of the individual as dependent on society for the means of full development. The liberal democratic acceptance of economic and political inequality has been shown to be inconsistent with democracy conceived as providing maximum opportunities for *all* persons to develop their potentials. Finally, Macpherson certainly would advocate the following interlocking propositions: (1) that government can and should protect the common interests of all citizens; and (2) that government should therefore have the capacity to act in defense of that common interest.

In short, the way of life envisioned by Macpherson is emphatically more democratic than liberal democracy, and comes much closer than liberal democracy to congruence with Iberian traditions. It is compatible, in fact, with a democratic version of those traditions. We are thereby able to move far toward dealing with a problem cited earlier in this chapter: the fact that Latin American culture as we know it reflects and serves the more privileged sectors of society, while it deceives and oppresses the mass of workers and peasants. In a developmental and participatory democracy, since all would have equal access to the means for development of their capacities, a humanistic culture would emerge which would reflect the participation of all: there would be no privileged sectors.

We noted a critical problem that Macpherson has not solved: is there any necessary content to his notion of the development of human capacities? Of course, no one is entitled to interfere with the developmental opportunities of others, but beyond that, have we any criteria to distinguish wholesome from unwholesome development, good development from better? Liberal societies, with their deeply rooted tradition of freedom of conscience, are probably less able to deal with this problem than the profoundly Catholic societies of Latin America. What is involved here is not particularly the role of the church as an institution, a role which is exceedingly complex and ambiguous. Rather, we are speaking of a characteristic mode of thinking and discourse in which it is taken for granted that questions of value are not merely matters of opinion, that they can and should be dealt with in terms set by widely held fundamental principles. In Latin America agreement on fundamental principles is a norm imperfectly realized, while in liberal North Atlantic societies such agreement is not expected or even desired.

Thus even though in practice Latin American societies do not agree on fundamental principles, Latin Americans are on the whole better equipped than North Americans to deal with the question of what sort of human development is best (compare Galston, 1982).

What would a Latin American democracy look like? Most obviously, economic power would have to approach an egalitarian distribution. Some private ownership of the means of production could be maintained, but there would also have to be measures to prevent the reconcentration of economic power. Certainly major corporations would have to be broken up. The role of transnational corporations is a particular problem in Latin America because such corporations have a huge impact in each country, yet are essentially beyond the control of any country. Because no Latin American country can extricate itself from the world capitalist economy, none can be totally rid of transnational corporations. But for democracy to be achieved, the influence of transnationals in the economy and polity must be severely limited. One possible device would be to prohibit them from owning or operating any enterprise other than one involved exclusively in imports and exports. Such a measure would prevent transnationals from dominating the internal economy, while acknowledging their inevitable role in international commerce.

The positive corollary to eliminating the concentration of economic power must be the organization of the economy for efficient participatory management. Agricultural smallholdings, if well-managed and of efficient size, could be left in individual hands, as could small commercial and handicraft firms. Operations most efficiently carried on by more than one worker should be organized on the basis of ownership and management by the workers themselves. When operation on a huge scale is necessary (for example, in a steel mill) a more elaborate management structure would be needed, the more adequately to serve the worker-owners (compare Markovic, 1982).

All workers, as an aspect of participating in the management of their firms, would be involved in an ongoing process of coordination and planning of the national economy. This process should be able, when necessary, to generate clear decisions binding on the firms involved. This would be an infringement on the autonomy of the firms, but it would seem necessary if the economy were to operate efficiently in the interests of the whole society.

An economy shaped thus would make possible a democratic polity as well. These democratizing economic changes would negate or weaken all of the major participants in existing liberal democratic accommodations, and would thus make possible the replacement of the existing elite corporatism by a popular corporatism based in the decentralized and participatory economic system. The various sectors of the economy would naturally need to organize themselves for participation in the elaborate process of coordination and planning already alluded to. In the absence of significant concentrations of economic power, however, the interdependence of the sectors would be far more important than any conflicts of interest between them. All interests consistent with the humanistic and developmental premises of the democratic regime would be full participants.

The principles of decentralization and participatory decision-making would militate against the emergence of dominating elites in such a system. On the other hand, as already noted, there would be a need for some sort of binding coordination and planning, an imperative which would tend to generate an elite. There is no easy answer to this dilemma, no way to assure that democracy will not degenerate, but a combination of factors may work against such a development. A process of coordination and planning that entailed a great deal of two-way communication between sectors and with the center would tend to retard the concentration of decision-making power. The decentralized structure of power itself, of course, would be resistant to recentralization. Finally, the maintenance of a democratic society, as much as liberal democracy, would require a conscious commitment of participants to its nurture.

# *Notes*

## Chapter 2

1. Outstanding general interpretations of Colombian political history and political economy include Guillén Martínez (1979); essays by Jaramillo Uribe, Melo, Tirado Mejía, and Arrubla in Arrubla et al. (1979); Safford (1977); essay by Solaún in Berry et al. (1980); Hartlyn (1981).

2. On nineteenth century Colombian economic history, see especially McGreevey (1971); Urrutia and Arrubla, eds. (1970); Bergquist (1978); Palacios (1980); Safford (1977); Leal Buitrago et al. (1977); Urrutia (1972); Tirado Mejía (1975); Nieto Arteta (1970, 1975); Ospina Vásquez (1955); Machado (1977); Melo (1979).

3. In addition to sources cited previously, for twentieth century Colombian economic history, see essays by Bejarano and Kalmanowitz, in Arrubla et al. (1979); Wright (1980).

4. The classic early study is Guzmán Campos et al. (1980). The most systematic recent study is Oquist (1980). See also Fluharty (1957); Martz (1962); Posada (1968) and an additional voluminous literature.

5. General sources for the history of Costa Rica include Monge Alfaro (1980); Vega Carballo (1979); Cardoso and Pérez-Brignoli (1977); Meléndez (1977); Ameringer (1982). Arguments of this section are developed more fully in Peeler (1982), pp. 1–56.

6. See especially Baires (1975); Stone (1975); Vega Carballo (1981b); Facio (1975); Hall (1978); Moretzsohn de Andrade (1974); Churnside (1978); Cardoso (1973); Cardoso and Pérez-Brignoli (1977).

7. Stone (1975), pp. 215–21. The census of 1883 indicated that 12 percent of the population could read but not write, and 15 percent could read *and* write. (Costa Rica, Ministerio de Economía, Industria y Comercio, 1975, p. 90).

8. For this period, see especially Vega Carballo (1981a), pt. 4, and (1981b), chap. 10; Stone (1975), chap. 8; Cardoso and Pérez-Brignoli (1977), chaps. 8–9; Monge Alfaro (1980), chaps. 9–13; Araya Pochet, in Aguilar Bulgarelli (1971); Hall (1978), chap. 2.

9. See Salazar Mora (1981), pp. 47–60; Schifter, in Zelaya, ed., (1979), I:48; Aguilar Bulgarelli in Zelaya (1981), pp. 50–62; Monge Alfaro (1980), pp. 291–93; Volio (1972); Vega Carballo (1979), pp. 36–37.

10. Good sources for 1940–49 include Aguilar Bulgarelli, in Zelaya (1981), pp. 6–63; Aguilar Bulgarelli (1974), p. 26; Aguilar Bulgarelli

(1977), pp. 6off.; Schifter (1979), p. 48; Salazar Mora (1974); Bell (1971); Navarro Bolandi (1957); Salazar Mora (1981); Rojas Bolaños (1980); Cañas (1955).

11. Compare Aguilar Bulgarelli (1974), pp. 47–49; and Schifter (1979), pp. 62ff. The "social guarantees" included a minimum wage, an eight hour workday, legal recognition of unions, minimum conditions of hygiene and safety, the right of the worker to a state education, and priority of national workers over foreigners.

12. On the Partido Social Demócrata and its predecessors, see especially Araya Pochet (1968); English (1971); Aguilar Bulgarelli (1974); Cañas (1955); Navarro Bolandi (1957); Schifter (1979); Schifter, in Zelaya (1981).

13. General sources on the history of Venezuela include Salcedo-Bastardo (1979); Lombardi (1982); and, for economic and social history, Brito Figueroa (1978).

14. On the colonial economy, see Brito Figueroa (1978), vol. 1; Malavé Mata (1975); Carvallo and de Hernández (1979b); Arellano Moreno (1973). On the Independence period and early nineteenth century, see Izard (1976), pp. 1–31; Mijares (1975), pp. 23–173; Ríos de Hernández (1976).

15. See Juan Uslar Pietri (1975). Compare Harwich Vallenilla (1976); Izard (1976); See also Frankel (1976), pp. 129–62; and Matthews (1976), pp. 91–127.

16. On the Gómez regime, see especially Gilmore (1965); Rangel (1975); Rangel (1964); Betancourt (1979); Clinton (1936); Gallegos Ortiz (1960); Sullivan (1976), pp. 247–71. For a contemporaneous justification of the regime, see the classic by Vallenilla Lanz (1952).

17. For an overview of the post-Gómez period, see Mayobre (1976), pp. 273–92; and Velásquez (1979). Useful analyses of the emergence of democracy in this period include Sonntag (1979); Carvallo and de Hernández (1979a); Irazábal (1974); Peeler (1977); Taylor (1971).

18. On post-Gómez economic development, see A. Uslar Pietri (1958); Izard (1970); Venezuela, Banco Central (1971); Salcedo-Bastardo (1979); Hanson (1977); Lieuwen (1954); Tugwell (1975).

## Chapter 3

1. General sources on contemporary Costa Rican politics include Denton (1971); Denton (1979); Zelaya (1979); English (1971); Stone (1975); Ameringer (1978); Ameringer (1982); Zelaya et al. (1981); Vega Carballo (1981b); Arias Sanchez (1978). General sources on contemporary Colombian politics include Berry et al. (1980); Leal Buitrago (1974); Latorre (1974); Latorre (1980); Dix (1967); Dix (1980); Hoskin et

al. (1976); Hartlyn (1981); Kline (1983); Ogliastri (1983). General sources on contemporary Venezuelan politics include Martz and Myers, eds., (1977); Martz (1966); Bonilla and Silva Michelena (1967); Bonilla (1970); Silva Michelena (1971); Martz and Baloyra (1976); Baloyra and Martz (1979); Alexander (1982); Herman (1980); Salcedo-Bastardo (1979); Blank (1973); Blank (1984); Silva Michelena and Sonntag (1979); Penniman, ed., (1980).

2. On political participation, see Martz and Baloyra (1976); Baloyra and Martz (1979); Silva Michelena (1971); Weiss (1968); Murillo and Rivera Ortiz (1973); Losada and Williams (n.d.); Losada and Murillo (1973); Murillo and Williams (1975); Peeler (1976); Peeler (1977); Campos and McCamant (1972); Stone (1975); Carvajal Herrera (1978); Gómez (1977); Costa Rica, Casa Presidencial (1978); Booth and Seligson (1978); Seligson and Booth (1979).

3. See especially Arias Sánchez (1980); Silva Michelena (1971); Bonilla (1970); Martz and Myers (1977) chap. 7; Gil Yepes (1980); Guillén Martínez (1979).

4. AD and COPEI have followed quite different trajectories toward this accommodation. In the 1940s AD was the main organized force calling for social democratic reforms; thus, economic elites rejoiced at the overthrow of AD in 1948. The party's dominant leadership, centered around Rómulo Betancourt, enforced a moderation of its reformism after 1958, at the cost of losing the party's left wing. COPEI, in the 1940s, was a major supporter of the interests of the economic elite; the party supported the coup against AD in 1948 and broke with Pérez Jiménez quite late. Rafael Caldera led the party into its accommodation with AD as part of a transformation into a mass-based, centrist party less directly representative of business interests. See Martz (1966); Herman (1980); Kolb (1974).

5. See, for example, Ray (1969); Silva Michelena (1971); Baloyra and Martz (1979); Havens and Flinn (1970); Costa Rica, Casa Presidencial (1978); Booth and Seligson (1979); Richard and Meléndez, eds. (1982).

6. Major sources on contemporary economy and society in Colombia include part 2 of Berry et al. (1980); chapters by Bejarano and by Kalmanovitz, in Arrubla, et al. (1979); and Sorpa (1976). On Costa Rica, see several essays in Zelaya (1979); and Araya Pochet (1976). On Venezuela, see especially Brito Figueroa (1978), vol. 3; several chapters in Martz and Myers, eds. (1977); and many of the essays in *Venezuela 1979* (1980).

7. On Colombia, see especially Havens and Flinn (1970). On Costa Rica, see Costa Rica, Casa Presidencial (1978); Seligson and Booth, eds. (1979), chap. 6; Booth and Seligson, eds. (1978), chap. 9; Richard and Meléndez, eds. (1982), pp. 251–300. On Venezuela, see Ray (1969); Silva Michelena (1971).

## Chapter 4

1. For examples of this spirit of accommodation in Colombia, see Arrubla et al. (1979); and Latorre (1980). It is exemplified in Venezuela by the essays in *Venezuela 1979* (1980). See also the narrative in Alexander (1982) and various essays in Martz and Myers (1977). Examples of such discourse in Costa Rica are contained in Oduber et al. (1981); and Amador (1981).

2. On Uruguay, see Weinstein (1975); Kaufman (1979); and González (1983). Of the voluminous literature on Chile, see in particular Petras (1969); Kinsbruner (1973); Valenzuela (1978); and Valenzuela and Valenzuela (forthcoming). For a comparative analysis, see Peeler (1983).

3. See Castles (1978). On Sweden, see Rustow (1955); Scott (1977); Hancock (1972); and Levin, et al. (1972). On Norway, see Valen and Katz (1964); and Derry (1973).

4. For example, in Venezuela today, the range of realistic electoral alternatives includes AD and COPEI, whereas MAS and MIR are tolerated on the fringe of legal opposition, but not considered seriously. That status itself retards their ability to build popular support. After a hypothetical democratizing transition, we may imagine MAS and MIR as the realistic alternatives, AD and COPEI as the tolerated but irrelevant extreme right.

# References

Aguilar Bulgarelli, Oscar, coordinator. (1971) *El desarrollo nacional en 150 años de vida independiente*. San José: Universidad de Costa Rica, Serie histórica y geográfica No. 12.

_____. (1974) *Costa Rica y sus hechos políticos de 1948*. Second ed. San José: Ed. Universitaria Centroamericana—EDUCA.

_____. (1977) *Evolución histórica de una democracia*. Heredia: Universidad Nacional.

Alexander, Robert J. (1982) *Rómulo Betancourt and the Transformation of Venezuela*. New Brunswick: Transaction.

Almond, Gabriel A., Scott C. Flanagan, and Robert J. Mundt, eds. (1973) *Crisis, Choice, and Change: Historical Studies of Political Development*. Boston: Little, Brown.

_____, and Sidney Verba. (1963) *The Civic Culture*. Princeton: Princeton University Press.

Amador, Eduardo. (1981) "Proponen soluciones para fortalecer la democracia." *La Nación* (San José), 13 April.

Ameringer, Charles D. (1978) *Don Pepe: A Political Biography of José Figueres of Costa Rica*. Albuquerque: University of New Mexico Press.

_____. (1982) *Democracy in Costa Rica*. New York: Praeger.

Araya Pochet, Carlos. (1968) *Historia de los partidos políticos: Liberación Nacional*. Thesis, Licenciado en historia, Universidad de Costa Rica.

_____. (1976) *Historia económica de Costa Rica, 1950–1970*. Second ed. San José: Ed. Fernandez Arce.

Arellano Moreno, Antonia. (1973) *Orígenes de la economía venezolana*. Third ed. Caracas: Universidad Central de Venezuela.

Arias Sánchez, Oscar. (1978) *¿Quién gobierna en Costa Rica?* Second ed. San José: EDUCA.

_____. (1980) *Grupos de presión en Costa Rica*. Fifth ed. San José: Ed. Costa Rica.

Arrubla, Mario, et al. (1979) *Colombia, hoy*. Fourth ed. Bogotá: Siglo XXI.

Backer, James. (1975) *La iglesia y el sindicalismo en Costa Rica*. Second ed. San José: Ed. Costa Rica.

Baires, Yolanda. (1975) *Las transacciones inmobiliarias en el Valle Central y la expansión cafetalera de Costa Rica, 1800–1850*. Thesis, Licenciada en Sociología, Universidad de Costa Rica.

Baloyra, Enrique, and John Martz. (1979) *Political Attitudes in Venezuela: Societal Cleavages and Public Opinion.* Austin: University of Texas Press.

Barker, Ernest, ed. (1962) *Social Contract.* New York: Oxford University Press.

Bay, Christian. (1965) "Politics and Pseudopolitics." *American Political Science Review* 59:39–51.

Belaúnde, Víctor Andrés. (1966) *Bolívar and the Political Thought of the Spanish American Revolution.* Second ed. Baltimore: Johns Hopkins University Press.

Bell, John Patrick. (1971) *Crisis in Costa Rica: The Revolution of 1948.* Austin: University of Texas Press.

Bendix, Reinhard. (1978) *Kings or People: Power and the Mandate to Rule.* Berkeley: University of California Press.

Bergquist, Charles W. (1978) *Coffee and Conflict in Colombia, 1886–1910.* Durham: Duke University Press.

Berlin, Isaiah. (1969) *Four Essays on Liberty.* Oxford: Oxford University Press.

Bernstein, Richard J. (1976) *The Restructuring of Social and Political Theory.* Philadelphia: University of Pennsylvania Press.

Berry, R. Albert, et al. (1980) *Politics of Compromise: Coalition Government in Colombia.* New Brunswick: Transaction.

Betancourt, Rómulo. (1979) *Venezuela: Oil and Politics.* Boston: Houghton Mifflin.

Blank, David Eugene. (1973) *Politics in Venezuela.* Boston: Little, Brown.

———. (1984) *Venezuela: Politics in a Petroleum Republic.* New York: Praeger.

Bollen, Kenneth A. (1980) "Issues in the Comparative Measurement of Political Democracy." *American Sociological Review* 45:370–90.

Bonilla, Frank. (1970) *The Failure of Elites.* Vol. 2 of *The Politics of Change in Venezuela.* Cambridge: MIT Press.

———, and José A. Silva Michelena, eds. (1967) *A Strategy for Research on Social Policy.* Vol. 1 of *The Politics of Change in Venezuela.* Cambridge: MIT Press.

Booth, John, and Mitchell Seligson, eds. (1978) *Political Participation in Latin America,* vol. 1. New York: Holmes and Meier.

———. (1979) "Peasants as Activists: A Reevaluation of Political Participation in the Countryside." *Comparative Political Studies* 12:29–60.

Brito Figueroa, Federico. (1978) *Historia económica y social de Venezuela.* Three vols. Caracas: Universidad Central de Venezuela.

Bryce, James. (1891) *The American Commonwealth.* New York: Macmillan.

Burggraaff, Winfield J. (1972) *The Venezuelan Armed Forces in Politics, 1935–1959*. Columbia: University of Missouri Press.

Busey, James L. (1962) *Notes on Costa Rican Democracy*. Boulder: University of Colorado.

Campos, Judith Talbot, and John F. McCamant. (1972) *Cleavage Shift in Colombia: Analysis of the 1970 Elections*. Professional Papers in Comparative Politics, No. 01-032. Beverly Hills: Sage.

Cañas, Alberto F. (1955) *Los 8 años*. San José: Ed. Liberación Nacional.

Cardoso, Ciro. (1973) "La formación de la hacienda cafetalera en Costa Rica (siglo XIX)." *Estudios Sociales Centroamericanos* no. 6 (September–December), pp. 22–50.

_____, and Héctor Pérez-Brignoli. (1977) *Centroamerica y economía occidental (1520–1930)*. San José: Ed. Universidad de Costa Rica.

Carvajal Herrera, Mario. (1978) *Actitudes políticas del costarricense: Análisis de opinión de dirigentes y partidarios*. San José: Ed. Costa Rica.

Carvallo, Gastón, and Josefina de Hernández. (1979a) "Dominación burguesa y democracia representativa en Venezuela: Apuntes para la evaluación de funcionamiento." Paper, XIII Congreso Latinoamericano de Sociología, Panamá.

_____. (1979b) "Economía cafetalera y clase dominante en Venezuela (1830–1920)." In *Agricultura y sociedad: Tres ensayos históricos*. Caracas: Universidad Central, CENDES (unpublished).

Castles, Francis G. (1978) *The Social Democratic Image of Society*. London: Routledge & Kegan Paul.

Castro Esquivel, Arturo. (1955) *José Figueres Ferrer, el hombre y su obra*. San José: Emprenta Torma.

Cavarozzi, Marcelo. (1982) "Argentina at the Crossroads: Pathways and Obstacles to Democratization in the Present Political Conjuncture." Working Paper No. 115. Washington: Wilson Center, Latin American Program.

Churnside, Roger. (1978) "Concentración de la tierra en Costa Rica en 1935 y 1800–1850: algunas consideraciones de tipo metodológica." San José: Universidad de Costa Rica.

Clinton, Daniel Joseph. (1936) *Gómez: Tyrant of the Andes*. New York: Morrow.

Cnudde, Charles, and Deane E. Neubauer, eds. (1969) *Empirical Democratic Theory*. Chicago: Markham.

Colombia, Registraduría Nacional del Estado Civil. (1974) *Estadísticas electorales, abril 21, 1974*. Bogotá: RNEC.

_____. (1978) *Estadísticas electorales, 4 de junio de 1978*. Bogotá: RNEC.

_____. (1982) Boletines 23, 24, 36. Bogotá: RNEC.

Costa Rica, Casa Presidencial. (1978) *Opiniones y expectativas sobre el nuevo gobierno en abril de 1978.* San José: Casa Presidencial.

——. (1982) *La Gaceta,* nos. 43 (3 March) and 55 (22 March). San José: Government Printing Office.

——, Ministerio de Economía, Industria y Comercio. (1975) *Censo de población.* San José: Ministerio de Economía, Industria y Comercio.

——, Tribunal Supremo de Elecciones. (1969) *Cómputo de votos y declaratorias de elección, 1953, 1958, 1962, 1966.* San José: TSE.

——. (1970) *Cómputo . . . 1970.* San José: TSE.

——. (1974) *Cómputo . . . 1974.* San José: TSE.

——. (1978) *Cómputo . . . 1978.* San José: TSE.

Coulter, Phillip. (1975) *Social Mobilization and Liberal Democracy.* Lexington: Heath.

Dahl, Robert A. (1956) *A Preface to Democratic Theory.* Chicago: University of Chicago Press.

——. (1961) *Who Governs?* New Haven: Yale University Press.

——. (1970) *After the Revolution?* New Haven: Yale University Press.

——. (1971) *Polyarchy.* New Haven: Yale University Press.

——. (1978) "Pluralism Revisited." *Comparative Politics* 10:191–203.

——. (1982) *Dilemmas of Pluralist Democracy.* New Haven: Yale University Press.

Dahrendorf, Ralf. (1979) *Society and Democracy in Germany.* Second ed. New York: Norton.

Davis, Harold Eugene. (1972) *Latin American Thought: A Historical Introduction.* Baton Rouge: Louisiana State University Press.

Denton, Charles F. (1971) *Patterns of Costa Rican Politics.* Boston: Allyn and Bacon.

——. (1979) "Costa Rica." In Howard J. Wiarda and Harvey Kline, eds., *Latin American Politics and Development.* Boston: Houghton Mifflin.

Derry, T. K. (1973) *A History of Modern Norway, 1814–1972.* Oxford: Oxford University Press.

DiBacco, Thomas V., ed. (1977) *Presidential Power in Latin American Politics.* New York: Praeger.

Dix, Robert H. (1967) *Colombia: The Political Dimensions of Change.* New Haven: Yale University Press.

——. (1980) "Consociational Democracy: The Case of Colombia." *Comparative Politics* 12:303–21.

Duncan, Graeme, ed. (1983) *Democratic Theory and Practice.* Cambridge: Cambridge University Press.

Duverger, Maurice. (1963) *Political Parties.* New York: Wiley.

——. (1974) *Modern Democracies: Economic Power versus Political Power.* Hinsdale, Ill.: Dryden.

Eckstein, Harry. (1966) *Division and Cohesion in Democracy*. Princeton: Princeton University Press.

English, Burt H. (1971) *Liberación Nacional in Costa Rica: The Development of a Political Party in a Transitional Society*. Gainesville: University of Florida Press.

Facio, Rodrigo. (1975) "Estudio sobre economía costarricense." *Obras de Rodrigo Facio*. Second ed., vol. I, pp. 23–187. San José: Ed. Costa Rica.

*The Federalist*. (N.d.) New York: Modern Library.

Fierro, Lourdes, and Yostón Ferrigni. (1978) "Prediagnóstico sociohistórico de Venezuela, Fase III: El proceso de estructuración capitalista de la formación social venezolana." Caracas: Universidad Central de Venezuela, CENDES (unpublished).

Figueres, José. (1955) *Palabras gastadas*. San José: Imprenta Nacional.

Finer, S. E. (1975) *The Man on Horseback*. Second ed. New York: Penguin.

Fluharty, Vernon. (1957) *Dance of the Millions: Military Rule and the Social Revolution in Colombia, 1930–1956*. Pittsburgh: University of Pittsburgh Press.

Frankel, Benjamin A. (1976) "La Guerra Federal y sus sequelas, 1859–1869." In *Política y economía en Venezuela, 1810–1976*, pp. 129–62. Caracas: Fundación John Boulton.

Gallegos Ortiz, Rafael. (1960) *La historia política de Venezuela de Cipriano Castro a Pérez Jiménez*. Caracas: Imprenta Universitaria.

Galston, William. (1982) "Defending Liberalism." *American Political Science Review* 76:621–29.

Gilmore, Robert L. (1965) *Caudillism and Militarism in Venezuela, 1830–1910*. Athens: Ohio University Press.

Gil Yepes, José Antonio. (1981) *The Challenge of Venezuelan Democracy*. New Brunswick: Transaction.

Gómez B., Miguel, et al. (1977) *Informe general de la encuesta en zonas marginales del Area Metropolitana de San José—1977*. San José: Casa Presidencial.

González, Luis E. (1983) "Uruguay, 1980–1981: An Unexpected Opening." *Latin American Research Review* 18, no. 3: 63–76.

Gramsci, Antonio. (1971) *Selections from the Prison Notebooks*. New York: International.

Green, Thomas Hill. (1885) *Works*. London: Longmans.

Guillén Martínez, Fernando. (1979) *El poder político en Colombia*. Bogotá: Punta de Lanza.

Guzmán Campos, Germán, et al. (1980) *La violencia en Colombia*. 2 vols., ninth ed. Bogotá: Carlos Valencia Eds.

Habermas, Jürgen. (1971) *Knowledge and Human Interests*. Boston: Beacon.

Hall, Carolyn. (1978) *El café y el desarrollo histórico y geográfico de*

*Costa Rica*. San José: Ed. Costa Rica and Ed. Universidad Nacional.

Hammergren, Linn A., ed. (1983) *Development and the Politics of Administrative Reform*. Boulder: Westview.

Hancock, M. Donald. (1972) *Sweden: The Politics of Postindustrial Change*. Hinsdale, Ill.: Dryden.

Hanson, James A. (1977) "Cycles of Economic Growth and Structural Change since 1950." In John D. Martz and David J. Myers, eds. *Venezuela: The Democratic Experience*. New York: Praeger.

Hartlyn, Jonathan. (1981) *Consociational Politics in Colombia: Confrontation and Accommodation in Comparative Perspective*. Ph.D. dissertation, Yale University.

Harwich Vallenilla, Nikita. (1976) "El modelo económico del Liberalismo Amarillo: Historia de un fracaso, 1888–1908." In *Política y economía en Venezuela, 1810–1976*, pp. 203–46. Caracas: Fundación John Boulton.

Havens, A. Eugene, and William L. Flinn, eds. (1970) *Internal Colonialism and Structural Change in Colombia*. New York: Praeger.

Herman, Donald L. (1980) *Christian Democracy in Venezuela*. Chapel Hill: University of North Carolina Press.

Hobbes, Thomas. (1950) *Leviathan*. New York: Dutton.

Hoskin, Gary, et al. (1976) *Legislative Behavior in Colombia*. Buffalo: State University of New York.

Huntington, Samuel P. (1957) *The Soldier and the State*. New York: Vintage.

————. (1968) *Political Order in Changing Societies*. New Haven: Yale University Press.

Immerman, Richard H. (1982) *The CIA in Guatemala*. Austin: University of Texas Press.

Irazábal, Carlos. (1974) *Hacia la democracia: Contribución al estudio de la historia económica-política-social de Venezuela*. Third ed. Caracas: Jose Agustín Catelá.

Izard, Miguel. (1970) *Series estadísticas para la historia de Venezuela*. Mérida: Universidad de los Andes.

————. (1976) "Período de la Independencia y la Gran Colombia." In *Política y economía en Venezuela, 1810–1976*, pp. 1–31. Caracas: Fundación John Boulton.

Jiménez Castro, Wilburg. (1977) *Análisis electoral de una democracia: Estudio del comportamiento politico costarricense durante el período 1953–1974*. San José: Ed. Costa Rica.

Kaufman, Edy. (1979) *Uruguay in Transition*. New Brunswick: Transaction.

Kinsbruner, Jay. (1973) *Chile: A Historical Interpretation*. New York: Harper & Row.

Kline, Harvey. (1983) *Colombia: Portrait of Unity and Diversity*. Boulder: Westview.

Kolb, Glen L. (1974) *Democracy and Dictatorship in Venezuela, 1945–1958*. Hamden: Archon.

Latorre, Mario. (1974) *Elecciones y partidos políticos en Colombia*. Bogotá: Universidad de los Andes.

_____. (1980) *Política y elecciones*. Bogotá: Universidad de los Andes.

Leal Buitrago, Francisco. (1974) *Análisis histórico del desarrollo político nacional, 1930–1970*. Bogotá: Tercer Mundo.

_____, et al. (1977) *El agro en el desarrollo histórico de Colombia*. Bogotá: Punta de Lanza.

Levin, Leif, et al. (1972) *The Swedish Electorate, 1887–1968*. Stockholm: Almqvist & Wiksell.

Levine, Andrew. (1981) *Liberal Democracy: A Critique of Its Theory*. New York: Columbia University Press.

Levine, Daniel H. (1981) *Religion and Politics in Latin America: The Catholic Church in Venezuela and Colombia*. Princeton: Princeton University Press.

Lieuwen, Edwin. (1954) *Petroleum in Venezuela: A History*. Berkeley: University of California Press.

Lijphart, Arend. (1977) *Democracy in Plural Societies: A Comparative Exploration*. New Haven: Yale University Press.

_____. (1984) *Democracies*. New Haven: Yale University Press.

Linz, Juan, and Alfred Stepan, eds. (1978) *The Breakdown of Democratic Regimes*. Baltimore: Johns Hopkins University Press.

Lively, Jack. (1977) *Democracy*. New York: Putnam.

Lombardi, John V. (1982) *Venezuela: The Search for Order, the Dream of Progress*. New York: Oxford University Press.

Losada, Rodrigo, and Gabriel Murillo. (1973) "Análisis de las elecciones de 1972 en Bogotá." Bogotá: Universidad de los Andes.

_____, and Miles W. Williams. (N.d.) "El voto presidencial en Bogotá: Análisis del comportamiento electoral del 19 de abril de 1970." Bogotá: Universidad de los Andes.

Lowell, A. Lawrence. (1892) *Essays on Government*. New York: Houghton Mifflin.

McBeth, B. S. (1983) *Juan Vicente Gómez and the Oil Companies in Venezuela, 1908–1935*. Cambridge: Cambridge University Press.

McCoy, Charles, and John Playford, eds. (1967) *Apolitical Politics: A Critique of Behavioralism*. New York: Crowell.

McGreevey, William Paul. (1971) *An Economic History of Colombia, 1845–1930*. Cambridge: Cambridge University Press.

Machado, Absalón. (1977) "Incidencias de la economía cafetera en el desarrollo rural." In Francisco Leal Buitrago, et al., *El agro en el desarrollo historico de Colombia*, pp. 179–228. Bogotá: Punta de Lanza.

Macpherson, C. B. (1973) *Democratic Theory: Essays in Retrieval*. Oxford: Oxford University Press.

———. (1977) *The Life and Times of Liberal Democracy*. Oxford: Oxford University Press.

Magallanes, Manuel Vicente. (1973) *Los partidos políticos: Evolución histórica venezolana*. Madrid: Ed. Mediterráneo Diego de León.

Malavé Mata, Hector. (1975) *Formación histórico del antidesarrollo de Venezuela*. Third ed. Caracas: Ed. Rocinante.

Malthus, Thomas. (1970) *An Essay on the Principle of Population*. New York: Penguin.

Manley, John. (1983) "Neopluralism: A Class Analysis of Pluralism I and Pluralism II." *American Political Science Review* 77: 368–83; comments by Lindblom and Dahl, 384–89.

Marcuse, Herbert. (1964) *One-Dimensional Man*. Boston: Beacon.

Markovic, Mihailo. (1982) *Democratic Socialism: Theory and Practice*. New York: St. Martin's.

Martz, John D. (1962) *Colombia: A Contemporary Political Survey*. Chapel Hill: University of North Carolina Press.

———. (1966) *Acción Democrática: Evolution of a Modern Political Party in Venezuela*. Princeton: Princeton University Press.

———, and Enrique Baloyra. (1976) *Electoral Mobilization and Public Opinion: The Venezuelan Campaign of 1973*. Chapel Hill: University of North Carolina Press.

———, and David J. Myers, eds. (1977) *Venezuela: The Democratic Experience*. New York: Praeger.

Marx, Karl. (1978) "Critique of the Gotha Program." In Robert C. Tucker, ed., *The Marx-Engels Reader*. Second ed., edited by Robert C. Tucker, pp. 525–41. New York: Norton.

Matthews, Robert P. (1976) "La turbulenta década de los Monagas." In *Política y economía en Venezuela, 1810–1976*, pp. 91–127. Caracas: Fundación John Boulton.

Maullin, Richard. (1973) *Soldiers, Guerrillas, and Politics in Colombia*. Lexington: Heath.

Mayobre, José Antonio. (1976) "Desde 1936 hasta nuestros dias." In *Política y economía en Venezuela, 1810–1976*, pp. 273–92. Caracas: Fundación John Boulton.

Meléndez, Carlos. (1977) *Costa Rica: Tierra y poblamiento en la colonia*. San José: Ed. Costa Rica.

Melo, Jorge Orlando. (1979) "La evolución económica de Colombia." In *Manual de Historia de Colombia*, vol. 2, pp. 133–210. Bogotá: Instituto Colombiano de Cultura.

*Mesoamerica*. (1984) 3 (4) San José: Institute for Central American Studies.

Mijares, Augusto. (1975) "La evolución política de Venezuela, 1810–1960." In Mariano Picón Salas, et al., *Venezuela independiente:*

*Evolución política y social, 1810–1960.* Caracas: Fundación Eugenio Mendoza.

Mill, John Stuart. (1975) *Three Essays: On Liberty, Representative Government, The Subjection of Women.* London: Oxford University Press.

Monge Alfaro, Carlos. (1980) *Historia de Costa Rica.* Sixteenth ed. San José: Librería Trejos.

Moore, Barrington. (1966) *Social Origins of Dictatorship and Democracy.* Boston: Beacon.

Moretzsohn de Andrade, F. (1974) "Decadencia del campesinado costarricense." In *El problema campesino y la concentración de la tierra en Costa Rica.* San José: CSUCA.

Murillo, Gabriel, and Israel Rivera Ortiz. (1973) *Actividades y estructura de poder de los partidos políticos colombianos.* Bogotá: Universidad de los Andes.

———, and Miles W. Williams. (1975) *Análisis de las elecciones presidenciales en 1974 en Bogota.* Bogotá: Universidad de los Andes.

Navarro Bolandi, Hugo. (1957) *La generación del 48.* Mexico: Ed. Humanismo.

Nieto Arteta, Luis Eduardo. (1970) *Economía y cultura en la historia de Colombia.* Medellín: Ed. La Oveja Negra.

———. (1975) *El café en la sociedad colombiana.* Bogotá: Ed. Tiempo Presente.

Nordlinger, Eric A. (1981) *On The Autonomy of the Democratic State.* Cambridge: Harvard University Press.

Ocampo, José Fernando. (1980) *Colombia siglo XX: Estudio histórico y antología politica,* vol. 1 (1886–1934). Bogotá: Tercer Mundo.

O'Donnell, Guillermo. (1979) *Modernization and Bureaucratic-Authoritarianism.* Second ed. Berkeley: University of California, Institute of International Studies.

Oduber, Daniel, et al. (1981) *Los problemas socio-políticos de desarrollo en Costa Rica.* San José: Ed. Universidad Estatal a Distancia.

Ogliastri, Enrique. (1983) "Estructura de poder y clases sociales: La democracia oligárquica en Colombia." Paper presented at the Latin American Studies Association, Mexico City.

Oquist, Paul. (1980) *Violence, Conflict, and Politics in Colombia.* New York: Academic Press.

Ospina Vásquez, Luis. (1955) *Industria y protección en Colombia, 1810–1930.* Medellín: Ed. Santa Fé.

Paine, Thomas. (1969) *The Rights of Man.* New York: Penguin.

———. (N.d.) *Common Sense.* New York: Penguin.

Palacios, Marco. (1980) *Coffee in Colombia, 1850–1970.* Cambridge:

Cambridge University Press.

Parry, Geraint. (1969) *Political Elites*. New York: Praeger.

Peeler, John A. (1976) "Colombian Parties and Political Development." *Journal of Inter-American Studies and World Affairs* 18:203–24.

———. (1977) *Urbanization and Politics*. Professional Papers in Comparative Politics, vol. 6, no. 01-062. Beverly Hills: Sage.

———. (1982) "Costa Rica." Unpublished paper. Bucknell University.

———. (1983) "The Conditions for Liberal Democracy in Latin America." Paper presented at the Latin American Studies Association, Mexico City.

Penniman, Howard R., ed. (1980) *Venezuela at the Polls: The National Elections of 1978*. Washington: American Enterprise Institute.

Pennock, J. Roland. (1979) *Democratic Political Theory*. Princeton: Princeton University Press.

Petras, James. (1969) *Politics and Social Forces in Chilean Development*. Berkeley: University of California Press.

Phelan, John L. (1978) *The People and the King: The Comunero Revolution in Colombia, 1781*. Madison: University of Wisconsin Press.

Posada, Francisco. (1968) *Colombia: Violencia y subdesarrollo*. Bogotá: n.p.

Poulantzas, Nicos. (1978) *State, Power, Socialism*. London: New Left Books.

Powell, G. Bingham. (1982) *Contemporary Democracies: Participation, Stability, and Violence*. Cambridge: Harvard University Press.

Rangel, Domingo Alberto. (1964) *Los andinos en el poder*. Mérida: Talleres Gráficos Universitarios.

———. (1975) *Gómez: El amo del poder*. Valencia: Vedell Hnos.

Rawls, John. (1971) *A Theory of Justice*. Cambridge: Harvard University Press.

Ray, Talton F. (1969) *The Politics of the Barrios of Venezuela*. Berkeley: University of California Press.

Richard, Pablo, and Guillermo Meléndez, eds. (1982) *La iglesia de los pobres en América Central*. San José: DEI.

Ríos de Hernández, Josefina. (1976) "Prediagnóstico sociohistórico de Venezuela, Fase II: El proceso de conformación, fraguado y crisis de la formación social venezolana." Caracas: Universidad Central, CENDES (unpublished).

Rivas Rivas, José, comp. (1961) *El mundo y la época de Pérez Jiménez*. Caracas: Pensamiento Vivo.

Rojas Bolaños, Manuel. (1980) *Lucha social y guerra civil en Costa Rica, 1940–1948*. San José: Ed. Porvenir.

Rosenberg, Mark. (1983) *Las luchas por el Seguro Social en Costa Rica*. San José: Ed. Costa Rica.

Ruhl, J. Mark. (1978) "Party System in Crisis? An Analysis of Colombia's 1978 Elections." *Inter-American Economic Affairs* 32, no. 3: 29–45.

———. (1980) *Colombia: Armed Forces and Society*. Syracuse: Syracuse University, Maxwell School of Citizenship and Public Affairs.

Rustow, Dankwart. (1955) *The Politics of Compromise: A Study of Parties and Cabinet Government in Sweden*. Princeton: Princeton University Press.

———. (1970) "Transitions to Democracy." *Comparative Politics* 2 (April): 337–63.

Safford, Frank. (1977) *Aspectos del siglo XIX en Colombia*. Medellín: Ed. Hombre Nuevo.

Salazar Mora, José Mario. (1974) *El Partido Republicano y la figura del Dr. Calderón Guardia*. Thesis, Historia y Geografía, Universidad de Costa Rica.

———. (1981) *Política y reforma en Costa Rica, 1914–1958*. San José: Ed. Porvenir.

Salcedo-Bastardo, J. L. (1979) *Historia fundamental de Venezuela*. Eighth rev. ed. Caracas: Universidad Central.

Schifter, Jacobo. (1979) *La fase oculta de la Guerra Civil en Costa Rica*. San José: EDUCA.

———. (1982) *Costa Rica 1948: Análisis de documentos confidenciales del Departamento de Estado*. San José: EDUCA.

Schmidt, Steffen W. (1974a) "Bureaucrats as Modernizing Brokers? Clientelism in Colombia." *Comparative Politics* 6:425–50.

———. (1974b) "La Violencia Revisited: The Clientelist Bases of Political Violence in Colombia." *Journal of Latin American Studies* 6:97–111.

———. (1974c) "The Transformation of Clientelism in Rural Colombia." Paper presented at the American Political Science Association, Chicago.

———. (1980) "Patrons, Brokers and Clients: Party Linkage in the Colombian System." In Kay Lawson, ed., *Political Parties and Linkages*. New Haven: Yale University Press.

Schoultz, Lars. (1981) *Human Rights and United States Policy toward Latin America*. Princeton: Princeton University Press.

Schumpeter, Joseph. (1962) *Capitalism, Socialism, and Democracy*. Third ed. New York: Harper & Row.

Scott, Franklin D. (1977) *Sweden: The Nation's History*. Minneapolis: University of Minnesota Press.

Seligson, Mitchell, and John Booth, eds. (1979) *Political Participation in Latin America*, vol. 2. New York: Holmes & Meier.

Sharpless, Richard E. (1978) *Gaitán of Colombia: A Political Biography*. Pittsburgh: University of Pittsburgh Press.

Silva Michelena, José A. (1971) *The Illusion of Democracy in Dependent Nations*. Vol. 3 of *The Politics of Change in Venezuela*. Cambridge: MIT Press.

————, and Heinz R. Sonntag. (1979) *El proceso electoral de 1978: Su perspectiva histórica estructural*. Caracas: Ed. Ateneo de Caracas.

Skinner, Quentin. (1973) "The Empirical Theorists of Democracy and Their Critics: A Plague on Both Their Houses." *Political Theory* 1:287–306.

Smith, Adam. (1970) *The Wealth of Nations*. New York: Penguin.

Sonntag, Heinz. (1979) "Reflexiones sobre la democracia en Venezuela." Caracas: Universidad Central, CENDES (unpublished).

Sorpa, Miguel. (1976) *Neoimperialismo y subdesarrollo colombiano*. Bogotá: Fundación Centro de Investigación y Educación Popular.

Soto, Sergio Reuben. (1982) *Capitalismo y crisis económica en Costa Rica*. San José: Ed. Porvenir.

Stein, Stanley J., and Barbara H. Stein. (1970) *The Colonial Heritage of Latin America: Essays on Economic Dependence in Perspective*. New York: Oxford University Press.

Stone, Samuel. (1975) *La dinastía de los conquistadores*. San José: EDUCA.

Sullivan, William M. (1976) "Situación económica y política durante el período de Juan Vicente Gómez, 1908–1935." In *Política y economía en Venezuela, 1810–1976*. Caracas: Fundación John Boulton.

Taylor, Philip. (1968) *The Venezuelan Golpe de Estado of 1958: The Fall of Marcos Pérez Jiménez*. Washington: Institute for the Comparative Study of Political Systems.

————. (1971) *Thoughts on Comparative Effectiveness: Leadership and the Democratic Left in Colombia and Venezuela*. Buffalo: State University of New York, Council on International Studies.

Therborn, Göran. (1979) "The Travail of Latin American Democracy." *New Left Review*, nos. 113–14, pp. 71–109.

Thompson, E. P. (1978) *The Poverty of Theory and Other Essays*. New York: Monthly Review.

Tirado Mejía, Alvaro. (1975) *Introducción a la historia económica de Colombia*. Fourth ed. Medellín: La Carreta.

Tocqueville, Alexis de. (1945) *Democracy in America*. 2 vols. New York: Vintage.

Truman, David B. (1971) *The Governmental Process*. Second ed. New York: Knopf.

Tugwell, Franklin. (1975) *The Politics of Oil in Venezuela*. Palo Alto: Stanford University Press.

United States Senate. (1975) *Covert Action in Chile, 1963–1973*. Staff report, Select Committee on Governmental Operations with Respect to Intelligence Activities. Washington: GPO.

Urrutia, Miguel. (1972) "El sector externo y la distribución de ingresos en Colombia en el siglo XIX." *Revista del Banco de la República* 45:1974–87.

————, and Mario Arrubla, eds. (1970) *Compendio de estadísticas históricas de Colombia*. Bogotá: Universidad Nacional.

Uslar Pietri, Arturo. (1958) *Sumario de economía venezolana*. Caracas: Fundación Eugenio Mendoza.

Uslar Pietri, Juan. (1975) *Historia política de Venezuela*. Second ed. Caracas: Ed. Mediterraneo.

Valen, Henry, and Daniel Katz. (1964) *Political Parties in Norway*. London: Tavistock.

Valenzuela, Arturo. (1978) *The Breakdown of Democratic Regimes: Chile*. Baltimore: Johns Hopkins University Press.

————, and J. Samuel Valenzuela. (forthcoming) *The Origins of Democracy: Reflections on the Chilean Case*. Cambridge: Cambridge University Press.

Vallenilla Lanz, Laureano. (1952) *Cesarismo democrático*. Caracas: Tipografía Garrido.

Vega Carballo, José Luis. (1979) "Las bases sociales de la democracia en Costa Rica." Paper presented at Center for Inter-American Relations, New York.

————. (1980) "Democracia y dominación en Costa Rica." *Foro Internacional* 20:646–72.

————. (1981a) *La formación del estado nacional en Costa Rica*. San José: Instituto Centroamericano de Administración Pública.

————. (1981b) *Hacia una interpretación del desarrollo costarricense: Ensayo sociológico*. Second ed. San José: Ed. Porvenir.

————. (1982) *Poder político y democracia en Costa Rica*. San José: Ed. Porvenir.

Velázquez, Ramón J., et al. (1979) *Venezuela moderna: Medio siglo de historia, 1926–1976*. Second ed. Caracas: Fundación Eugenio Mendoza.

————. (1981) "Por qué en el Táchira? Los comienzos de la industria petrolera venezolana." *El Nacional* (Caracas), 4 March, C1–2.

Véliz, Claudio. (1980) *The Centralist Tradition of Latin America*. Princeton: Princeton University Press.

Venezuela, Banco Central. (1971) *La economía venezolana: Los últimos 30 años*. Caracas: Banco Central.

————, Consejo Supremo Electoral. (1969) *Escrutinios de las elecciones, desde 1946 hasta 1968*. Caracas: CSE.

————. (1974) *Memoria y cuenta 1974*. Caracas: CSE.

————. (1978) *Resultado de las votaciones efectuadas el 3 diciembre 1978*. Caracas: CSE.

*Venezuela 1979: Exámen y Futuro*. (1980) Caracas: Ed. Ateneo de Caracas.

Verba, Sidney, Norman H. Nie, and Jae-On Kim. (1978) *Participation and Political Equality*. London: Cambridge University Press.

Volio, Marina. (1972) *Jorge Volio y el Partido Reformista*. San José: Ed. Costa Rica.

Weinstein, Martin. (1975) *Uruguay: The Politics of Failure*. Westport: Greenwood.

Weiss, Anita. (1968) *Tendencias de la participación electoral en Colombia, 1935–1966*. Bogotá: Universidad Nacional de Colombia.

Wesson, Robert. (1982) *Democracy in Latin America: Promise and Problems*. New York: Praeger.

Wiarda, Howard J., ed. (1980) *The Continuing Struggle for Democracy in Latin America*. Boulder: Westview.

———, ed. (1982) *Politics and Social Change in Latin America: The Distinct Tradition*. Second ed. Amherst: University of Massachusetts Press.

———, and Harvey Kline, eds. (1979) *Latin American Politics and Development*. Boston: Houghton Mifflin.

———, and Michael J. Kryzanek. (1982) *The Dominican Republic: A Caribbean Crucible*. Boulder: Westview.

Wilson, Woodrow. (1956) *Congressional Government*. New York: Meridian.

Wise, George S. (1951) *Caudillo: A Portrait of Antonio Guzmán Blanco*. New York: Columbia University Press.

Wright, Philip. (1980) "The Role of the State and the Politics of Capital Accumulation in Colombia." *Development and Change* 11:229–55.

Zelaya, Chester, ed. (1979) *Costa Rica contemporánea*. 2 vols. San José: Ed. Costa Rica.

———, et al. (1981) *¿Democracia en Costa Rica?*. San José: Ed. Universidad Estatal a Distancia.

# Index